Daily Morning Devotional for College Students

5-Minute Devotions To Empower Christian Men
During Their Studies

Biblical Teachings

CONTENTS

Let the Journey Begin...   VIII

NEW-FOUND INDEPENDENCE   1

1. Embracing Change   3

2. Developing Independence   6

3. Personal Responsibility   9

4. Effective Time Management   12

5. Building Life Skills   15

6. Creating a Routine   18

ACADEMICS   21

7. Studying with Purpose   22

8. The Power of Perseverance   25

9. Balancing Academics and Well-being   28

10. Managing Procrastination   31

11. Overcoming Comparison   34

12. Seeking Help and Support   37

SOCIAL LIFE   39

13. Identity and Peer Pressure   40

14. Peer Influence and Accountability   43

15. Building Meaningful Friendships   46

16. Overcoming Loneliness   49

17. Fostering Inclusivity   52

18. Social Media and Online Presence   55

19. Conflict Resolution   58

20. Respecting Boundaries   61

FINANCIAL MANAGEMENT   64

21. Stewardship   65

22. Budgeting Basics   68

23. Avoiding Debt   71

24. Part-Time Jobs and Financial Responsibility   74

25. Saving for the Future   77

26. Practicing Contentment   79

YOUR SPIRITUAL LIFE   82

27. Prioritizing Personal Devotions   83

28. Finding Community   86

29. Cultivating a Spirit of Gratitude   89

30. Integrating Faith and Learning   92

31. Overcoming Spiritual Dryness   95

32. The Power of Prayer   98

CAMPUS INVOLVEMENT   100

33. Stepping Out of Your Comfort Zone   101

34. Finding Your Niche and Strengths 104

35. Balancing Commitments 107

36. Overcoming Fear of Failure 110

37. Taking Advantage of College Resources 113

38. Exploring Interests and Passions 116

PHYSICAL HEALTH 119

39. Nurturing Physical and Mental Well-being in College 120

40. Fueling Your Body for Success 123

41. Fitness in College 125

42. Prioritizing Sleep 128

43. Screen Time 131

44. Substance Use and Abuse 134

MENTAL WELL-BEING 137

45. Embracing Rest and Sabbath 138

46. Practicing Self-Care 141

47. Developing Emotional Resilience 144

48. The Power of Your Thoughts 147

49. Navigating Stress and Anxiety 150

50. Seeking Professional Help 153

PERSONAL DEVELOPMENT 156

51. Embracing Self-Discovery 157

52. Cultivating Integrity and Moral Values 160

53. Adaptability 163

54. Developing Emotional Intelligence   166

55. Growing Self-Confidence   169

56. Building Leadership Skills   172

RELATIONSHIPS AND DATING   175

57. Balancing College Life and Home Connections   176

58. The Single Season   179

59. Seeking God's Guidance in Relationships   182

60. Building Emotional Intimacy   185

61. Healthy vs. Unhealthy Relationships   188

62. Balancing Friendships and Romantic Pursuits   191

SETTING GOALS   194

63. Goal Setting and Self-Reflection   195

64. Developing a Growth Mindset   198

65. Start with Small and Meaningful Goals   201

66. Overcoming Obstacles   204

67. Celebrating Milestones   207

68. Managing Expectations   210

GRADUATING WITH A KINGDOM MINDSET   213

69. Exploring Career Paths   214

70. Embracing Life Long Learning   217

71. Networking and Professional Relationships   219

72. Pursuing Internships and Experiential Learning   222

73. Dealing with Uncertainty   225

74. Graduating with a Kingdom Mindset   228

The Afterword   231

LET THE JOURNEY BEGIN...

College—the pinnacle of youth and adventure, where countless memories are made and dreams are forged. It's an exhilarating chapter of life filled with intense growth, new experiences, and the embrace of endless possibilities. But let's not forget, it can also be one of the most challenging periods you'll ever face.

As I reflect on my own college years, I realize they were far from perfect. Like many of us, I stumbled and made my fair share of mistakes. Yet, it is precisely these missteps that have shaped my understanding and propelled me to share my experiences with you. In the pages that follow, I offer you invaluable insights and lessons, drawing from both triumphs and trials, to help you navigate your own college journey with greater wisdom and grace.

Let me be clear—there's no magic formula to avoid every misstep or guarantee a flawless path. Mistakes are inevitable and often the catalysts for our most profound growth. However, my intention is to equip you with the tools, perspectives, and guidance necessary to make informed choices and maximize your college experience. Together, we'll navigate the maze of academia, friendships, spirituality, finances, relationships, and personal well-being, ensuring that your time in college is marked by both personal and spiritual growth.

Within these pages, you'll find stories that resonate with your own journey, intertwined with practical advice and timeless wisdom. We'll delve into the art of balancing newfound independence, mastering the delicate dance between academics and social life, and discovering the power of financial management. We'll explore the importance of nurturing your mental and physical health, keeping your spirituality alive, and building character that will carry you far beyond your college years. And yes, we'll unravel the mysteries of dating, relationships, and graduating with a kingdom mindset.

As you embark on this transformative journey, I invite you to open your heart and mind to the experiences of others. Approach each chapter with a hunger for knowledge, a desire to learn, and an openness to the possibilities that lie ahead. Together, we will navigate the intricacies of college life, armed with the wisdom and insights of those who have walked this path before us.

So, if you're ready to seize every opportunity, make informed decisions, and embrace the adventure that college presents, then this book is your faithful companion. Let it serve as your compass, guiding you through the challenges, triumphs, and discoveries that await. By the time you turn the final page, you'll be equipped with the knowledge and resilience to thrive academically, socially, and spiritually, not just during your college years, but for a lifetime.

Remember, life is indeed a balancing act, and if you can conquer it during your college experience, you'll set yourself up for a future of endless possibilities.

Your journey starts now...

NEW-FOUND
INDEPENDENCE

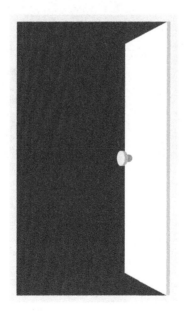

1

EMBRACING CHANGE

____ / ____ / _____

"For I know the plans I have for you, declares the Lord, plans for welfare and not for evil, to give you a future and a hope."

- JEREMIAH 29:11

As you embark on this new journey of college life, I want you to know that change can be both exciting and daunting. Just like you, I once stood at the threshold of uncertainty, unsure of what awaited me. It was a mix of emotions - anticipation, nervousness, and a longing for familiarity.

But let me assure you, God has a plan for your life. He knows the path He has set before you, and it is filled with hope and a future that is beyond what you can imagine. As you step into this new season, it's important to embrace the changes that come your way.

Consider the caterpillar transforming into a butterfly. In its initial stages, it may feel uncomfortable and unsure, but through the process of change, it emerges into something beautiful. Similarly, college life is a transformative journey that will shape you, challenge you, and help you discover the incredible potential within you.

One important lesson I learned during my college years is to lean on God in times of change. He is the constant amidst the shifting circumstances. When you feel overwhelmed or uncertain, seek His guidance and trust in His plan. Remember, He has brought you to this place for a purpose.

Embracing change also means stepping out of your comfort zone. College offers countless opportunities for personal growth, intellectual exploration, and forming new relationships. Don't be afraid to try new things, join clubs, engage in discussions, and meet people from diverse backgrounds. Embrace the unknown, for it is where you will discover your true potential and find joy in unexpected places.

How do you feel about the upcoming changes in your life as you transition to college?

Are there any specific fears or uncertainties you have about embracing change?

In what ways do you think college can help shape your future and bring hope?

How can you lean on God's guidance and trust in His plan during this transition?

What are some practical steps you can take to step out of your comfort zone and embrace new experiences in college?

Prayer:

Dear God,

As we embark on this new chapter of our lives, we pray for Your guidance and strength. Help us to embrace the changes that come with transitioning to college. Fill our hearts with hope and excitement for the future You have planned for us. Give us the courage to step out of our comfort zones and explore the opportunities that lie ahead. May we trust in Your unfailing love and rely on Your wisdom as we navigate this season of change. In Jesus' name, we pray.

Amen.

2

---◆◇◆---

DEVELOPING INDEPENDENCE

____ / ____ / _____

"For I can do everything through Christ, who gives me strength."

- PHILIPPIANS 4:13

College is a time of newfound independence where you have the opportunity to explore and develop your own identity. It's a journey of self-discovery, personal growth, and taking responsibility for your choices and actions. As you embark on this path, remember that true independence comes from relying on God's strength and guidance.

Think about a young bird leaving its nest for the first time. It flutters its wings, unsure of its ability to fly. But as it takes that leap of faith, it discovers its own strength and soars through the sky. Similarly, as a college student, you may feel a mix of excitement and uncertainty about the road ahead. Embrace this season as a chance to develop your independence and discover the gifts and potential within you.

Independence doesn't mean cutting ties with others or living solely for yourself. It means taking ownership of your decisions and embracing the responsibilities that come with them. It means learning to manage your time, set goals, prioritize, and make choices that align with your values and aspirations.

However, true independence isn't achieved by relying solely on your own strength. It's about recognizing that you are never alone in this journey. God is always by your side, ready to provide wisdom, guidance, and the strength to overcome any challenges you may face.

As you navigate this season of independence, remember to lean on God. Seek His will in your decisions and invite Him into every aspect of your life. Rely on His strength and trust that He will equip you with what you need to succeed.

Developing independence also involves learning from your experiences and seeking growth. Embrace new opportunities, step out of your comfort zone, and be open to learning from both successes and failures. Surround yourself with mentors, friends, and a supportive community that can walk alongside you, offering guidance and encouragement.

Remember, true independence comes when you surrender your plans and ambitions to God, allowing Him to shape your path. Trust in His unfailing love and believe that He has a purpose for your life. With His strength, you can navigate this journey of independence and thrive in all that you do.

In what areas of your life do you feel the need for greater independence? How can you seek God's guidance in those areas?

Reflect on a time when you took a step towards independence. How did it feel? What did you learn from that experience?

How can you balance independence with reliance on God's strength and guidance?

Prayer:

Dear God,

Thank You for the gift of independence and the opportunities it brings. As I navigate this season of college, help me to develop my independence while relying on Your strength and guidance. Teach me to make wise decisions, prioritize what is important, and trust in Your plan for my life. May my independence be rooted in faith and used to honor You.

Amen.

3

PERSONAL RESPONSIBILITY

____ / ____ / _____

"So then each of us will give an account of himself to God."

- ROMANS 14:12

During your college life, you will encounter countless opportunities and choices that will shape your experience. It's important to remember that personal responsibility plays a significant role in your growth and success during this time.

Let me share a personal experience that taught me the value of taking ownership of my choices. During my first year of college, I had the freedom to make my own decisions, and sometimes I made choices that were not aligned with my values. I neglected my responsibilities, procrastinated on assignments, and surrounded myself with negative influences. As a result, I faced consequences that affected my academic performance and overall well-being.

Through this experience, I realized that I had to take responsibility for my actions. I couldn't blame others or make excuses for my behavior. It was a humbling moment of self-reflection, where I recognized the need to make better choices and own up to the consequences they brought.

College is a time of growth, learning, and self-discovery. It's an opportunity to develop your character and become the person God has created you to be. Taking personal responsibility means recognizing that you have control over your choices and actions. It means understanding that your decisions have an impact not only on yourself but also on those around you.

As you navigate college life, ask yourself, "Am I taking ownership of my choices? Am I making decisions that align with my values and goals? Am I being accountable for the consequences of my actions?" Remember, you have the power to shape your college experience by making intentional and responsible choices.

How do you define personal responsibility, and why is it important in college life?

Can you recall a time when you took ownership of a mistake or poor choice? How did it impact your growth?

What are some common challenges you may face in taking personal responsibility in college?

Prayer:

Dear God,

We thank You for the gift of personal responsibility. Help us to understand the importance of owning our choices and actions. Grant us the wisdom to make decisions that align with Your will and our values. May we have the courage to take responsibility for the consequences of our actions and learn from our mistakes. Guide us on this journey of college life, so that we may grow into responsible and accountable individuals.

Amen.

4

---◄O►---

EFFECTIVE TIME MANAGEMENT

___ / ___ / _____

"Teach us to number our days, so that we may gain a heart of wisdom."

- PSALM 90:12

D avid was excited to embrace the new-found independence of college life. But he quickly realized that with freedom comes great responsibility, especially when it comes to managing his time effectively.

During his first semester, David struggled to balance his academic commitments, social activities, and personal interests. He often found himself cramming for exams, rushing to complete assignments, and feeling overwhelmed by the constant demands on his schedule.

One day, while reflecting on his chaotic routine, David came across the verse from Psalm 90:12. It served as a wake-up call, reminding him of the importance of valuing and wisely utilizing his time.

David learned that effective time management goes beyond simply filling every minute of the day with tasks. It's about setting priorities, creating a schedule that aligns with his goals and values, and making intentional choices.

He discovered the power of planning ahead, breaking tasks into smaller, manageable steps, and avoiding procrastination. He also recognized the significance of self-discipline, being mindful of time-wasting activities, and setting boundaries to protect his study time.

By implementing these strategies, David experienced a remarkable shift in his college journey. He found himself more focused, less stressed, and able to allocate time for both his academic pursuits and personal well-being.

Can you think of a time when poor time management affected your academic or personal life? How did it make you feel?

How can effective time management contribute to your overall success and well-being in college?

What are some practical steps you can take to improve your time management skills?

Prayer:

Dear God,

Thank You for the gift of time and the opportunity to make the most of each day. Grant us wisdom and guidance in managing our time effectively. Help us to prioritize our commitments, set boundaries, and make intentional choices. Teach us to use our time wisely, balancing our academic pursuits, personal growth, and spiritual well-being. May our time be a reflection of our dedication to You and our pursuit of excellence.

Amen.

BUILDING LIFE SKILLS

___ / ___ / _____

"Commit to the Lord whatever you do, and he will establish your plans."

- PROVERBS 16:3

A s you embark on your college journey, you have a wonderful opportunity not only to gain knowledge in your chosen field but also to develop valuable life skills that will serve you well beyond the classroom. Building life skills is about equipping yourself with the tools and abilities necessary to navigate various aspects of life with confidence and resilience.

Imagine a carpenter learning how to use different tools to construct a sturdy and beautiful structure. In the same way, college offers you a chance to acquire a toolbox of life skills. These skills may include effective communication, time management, problem-solving, decision-making, financial literacy, and adaptability.

Consider the importance of effective communication. Being able to express your thoughts and ideas clearly and respectfully can open doors to meaningful connections, collaborations, and opportunities.

Likewise, mastering time management skills will help you balance your academic commitments, extracurricular activities, and personal life, allowing you to make the most of your college experience.

Building life skills requires intentionality and practice. Seek opportunities within and outside the classroom to develop these skills. Join clubs or organizations that align with your interests, participate in team projects, volunteer, and take on leadership roles. Each experience will contribute to your growth and refinement.

Remember, God has entrusted you with unique gifts and abilities, and He desires for you to use them to make a positive impact in the world. As you commit your plans to Him and seek His guidance, He will empower you to develop the necessary skills to fulfill your purpose and serve others.

What life skills do you believe are important for your personal and professional development?

How can you actively work on developing those areas?

How can you involve God in your journey of building life skills? How can His wisdom and guidance shape your growth?

Prayer:

Dear God,

Thank You for the opportunities college offers me to build essential life skills. Guide me in recognizing areas where I can grow and equip me with the discipline and determination to develop these skills. Help me to commit my plans to You and seek Your guidance in all that I do. May the skills I acquire bring glory to Your name and be used for the betterment of others. In Jesus' name, I pray.

Amen.

CREATING A ROUTINE

____ / ____ / _____

"But seek first his kingdom and his righteousness, and all these things will be given to you as well."

- MATTHEW 6:33

College life can be filled with excitement, opportunities, and new experiences. As you navigate this season of newfound independence, it's important to establish a routine that promotes balance, productivity, and personal well-being. A well-designed routine can provide structure, reduce stress, and help you make the most of your college years.

Imagine you were a professional athlete preparing for a competition. You'd need to follow a carefully crafted routine that includes training, rest, nutrition, and mental preparation. Similarly, creating a routine in college can set you up for success in various areas of your life.

Start by identifying your priorities. What are your academic goals? What extracurricular activities do you want to participate in? How much time do you want to dedicate to personal hobbies, physical fitness, socializing, and spiritual growth? Once you have a clear vision of your priorities, you can design a routine that reflects and supports them.

Consider incorporating regular study blocks into your schedule to stay on top of your coursework. Allocate time for physical exercise to maintain your health and boost your energy levels. Set aside moments for self-reflection, prayer, and nurturing your relationship with God. Remember to include social activities to foster connections and create a sense of community.

While it's important to have structure in your routine, make sure to allow for flexibility. College life can be unpredictable, and unexpected opportunities or challenges may arise. Adaptability is key to maintaining a healthy balance. Be open to adjusting your routine when necessary while still honoring your commitments and priorities.

As you embark on this journey, remember to seek God's guidance in establishing your routine. Prioritize spending time with Him and seeking His will above all else. When you align your routine with His kingdom and righteousness, He promises to provide what you need to thrive academically, personally, and spiritually.

What are your top priorities in college? How can you incorporate them into your routine?

Reflect on a time when having a routine helped you stay focused and achieve your goals.

How can you involve God in your daily routine? In what ways can you seek His guidance and prioritize your relationship with Him?

Prayer:

Dear God,

Thank You for the gift of college and the opportunities it brings. As I create a routine, guide me in aligning my priorities with Your kingdom and righteousness. Help me to find balance, productivity, and fulfillment in my daily life. Grant me the wisdom to adapt when needed and the discipline to follow through with my commitments. May my routine reflect my desire to honor You in all that I do.

Amen.

ACADEMICS

7

---◆◇◆---

STUDYING WITH PURPOSE

____ / ____ / _____

"Whatever you do, work heartily, as for the Lord and not for men."

- COLOSSIANS 3:23

C ollege life brings with it academic challenges that require re-silience and determination. As a college student, you are constantly faced with the task of studying and preparing for exams. Developing effective study habits and strategies is essential for success in your academic journey.

Imagine this scenario: You have a major exam coming up, and you're feeling overwhelmed by the amount of material you need to cover. In times like these, it's important to study with purpose. Studying with purpose means approaching your academic responsibilities with intentionality and a focus on your goals.

One essential study habit is creating a structured study schedule. Set aside dedicated time each day for studying, ensuring that you allocate sufficient time for each subject. By following a schedule, you can establish a routine and avoid procrastination, which often leads to added stress and poor performance.

Another important strategy is setting clear goals for your study sessions. Identify what you want to accomplish during each session and break down larger tasks into smaller, manageable chunks. This approach helps you stay focused and motivated, as you can see your progress along the way.

While studying, it's crucial to create an environment conducive to learning. Find a quiet and comfortable space where you can concentrate without distractions. Minimize interruptions by turning off your phone or using apps that limit access to social media. This way, you can fully engage with your study materials and maximize your learning potential.

Remember that studying is not just about memorizing facts but also about understanding and applying concepts. Take active learning approaches, such as summarizing information in your own words, teaching it to others, or engaging in group discussions. These techniques deepen your understanding and enhance long-term retention.

As you study, keep in mind the verse from Colossians 3:23. Approach your studies as an opportunity to work heartily, not only for academic achievement but also as an act of worship to God. By adopting this perspective, you bring purpose and meaning to your academic pursuits, recognizing that your growth and development contribute to your overall purpose in God's plan for your life.

What study habits and strategies have you found effective in the past? How can you incorporate them into your current routine?

Reflect on a time when you faced a challenging academic situation. How did you overcome it, and what lessons did you learn from that experience?

Consider the environment in which you typically study. Is it conducive to learning, or are there distractions that hinder your focus? What changes can you make to create a more productive study space?

Prayer:

Dear God,

Thank You for the gift of education and the opportunities to learn and grow in college. As I strive to develop effective study habits and strategies, guide me in setting clear goals, managing my time, and creating a conducive study environment. Help me approach my studies with purpose, recognizing that my academic pursuits are not only for my own benefit but also for Your glory. Grant me wisdom, focus, and resilience to overcome challenges and excel in my academic journey.

Amen.

8

---◄○►---

THE POWER OF PERSEVERANCE

___ / ___ / _____

"Whatever you do, work at it with all your heart, as working for the Lord, not for human masters."

- COLOSSIANS 3:23

In the bustling lecture hall, Professor Johnson's voice filled the air, capturing the attention of the students. Among them was a young man named Daniel. As Daniel sat in his seat, he couldn't help but notice the genuine enthusiasm in the professor's words. The topic at hand was one he had never considered before—ancient civilizations. Normally, Daniel would have tuned out, allowing his mind to wander, but something was different this time.

As Professor Johnson spoke passionately about the wonders of the past, Daniel felt a spark of curiosity ignite within him. He began to see the subject in a new light, no longer viewing it as a mere requirement but as an opportunity to uncover hidden treasures of knowledge. The more he listened, the more he realized that every lecture held the potential to broaden his horizons and transform his understanding of the world.

Daniel's newfound perspective mirrored the story of King Solomon from the Bible. When God granted Solomon a wish, he chose wisdom above all else. Throughout his life, Solomon pursued knowledge and became known for his wisdom. In a similar vein, Daniel recognized the value of embracing learning not just as a means to an end but as a journey of personal growth and discovery.

The joy of learning, Daniel realized, comes from the active pursuit of knowledge. It's about approaching each subject with enthusiasm, embracing the challenges, and uncovering the beauty and wonder hidden within. As he embarked on this academic journey, Daniel understood that his studies were not just about grades or degrees but about developing critical thinking skills, expanding his perspectives, and nurturing a lifelong love for learning.

Finding joy in learning also meant aligning his studies with a greater purpose. Daniel realized that the knowledge he acquired could be used to serve others and make a positive impact in the world. Whether it was through solving complex problems or sharing insights with his peers, he recognized that his education was a gift to be stewarded for the betterment of society and the honor of God.

Think back to a moment when you experienced genuine joy in learning. What made that experience special or memorable for you?

Reflect on a subject or topic that you initially found uninteresting or challenging. How can you approach it with a fresh perspective and find joy in the process of understanding it?

In what ways can you view your education as an opportunity to honor and serve God? How can your studies contribute to your personal growth and your ability to make a difference in the world?

Prayer:

Dear God,

Thank You for the gift of knowledge and the opportunity to learn. Help me rediscover the joy of learning, not merely as a means to an end but as a pathway to growth, understanding, and service. Grant me a thirst for knowledge, a curious spirit, and an open mind. Teach me to approach my studies with passion and purpose, using the wisdom I gain to honor You and make a positive impact in the world. May the wonder of learning continue to shape and transform me.

Amen.

9

Balancing Academics and Well-being

____ / ____ / _____

"Do you not know that your bodies are temples of the Holy Spirit, who is in you, whom you have received from God? You are not your own."

- 1 Corinthians 6:19

In college, the demands of academics can often feel overwhelming. The pressure to excel academically can sometimes overshadow the importance of taking care of ourselves. Let me share a story to shed light on this.

Ethan was a college student passionate about his studies. He would spend countless hours in the library, pushing himself to the limit to achieve top grades. However, as the workload increased, Ethan's physical and mental well-being began to suffer. He would skip meals, sacrifice sleep, and neglect exercise, thinking that success in academics required sacrificing self-care.

One day, while reflecting on his situation, Ethan came across the verse from 1 Corinthians 6:19. It reminded him that his body is a temple of the Holy Spirit, a precious gift from God. Ethan realized that neglecting self-care was not a sign of dedication but rather a disregard for the gift he had been given.

This realization sparked a change in Ethan's approach. He started prioritizing self-care alongside his academic responsibilities. He ensured he got enough sleep, nourished his body with healthy meals, and made time for exercise and relaxation. Surprisingly, Ethan found that taking care of himself actually improved his focus, productivity, and overall well-being.

The story of Ethan teaches us the importance of prioritizing self-care for academic success. When we neglect our physical and mental well-being, our ability to excel academically diminishes. By embracing a healthy lifestyle and honoring our bodies as temples of the Holy Spirit, we create a foundation for holistic success.

So, as you navigate your college journey, remember to prioritize self-care. Take breaks, establish healthy routines, seek support when needed, and make time for activities that bring you joy and rejuvenation. By nurturing your well-being, you will find yourself better equipped to handle the academic challenges that come your way.

How do you currently prioritize self-care in your life? Are there areas where you can improve?

Reflect on a time when neglecting self-care negatively impacted your academic performance or overall well-being. What lessons did you learn from that experience?

How does recognizing your body as a temple of the Holy Spirit influence your perspective on self-care? In what ways can you honor and care for your body as a way of glorifying God?

Prayer:

Dear God,

Thank You for the gift of life and the opportunity to pursue education. Help me to remember that my body is a temple of Your Spirit, and I have a responsibility to care for it. Guide me in prioritizing self-care and balancing my academic pursuits with my physical and mental well-being. Grant me the wisdom to establish healthy routines and seek support when needed. May my pursuit of knowledge be accompanied by a commitment to nurture my overall well-being.

Amen.

10

MANAGING PROCRASTINATION

___/___/_____

"So teach us to number our days that we may get a heart of wisdom."

- PSALM 90:12

C ollege life can be filled with countless responsibilities and deadlines. It's easy to fall into the trap of procrastination, delaying
tasks until the last minute.

An old friend of mine named Alex struggled with procrastination.
Whenever he had assignments or projects, he would convince himself
that he had plenty of time to complete them. He would spend hours
on social media, watch videos, and engage in other distractions, be-
lieving he could always catch up later.

However, as the due dates approached, Alex found himself overwhelmed and stressed. He realized that his procrastination not only affected his academic performance but also caused unnecessary anxiety.
It was time for a change.

One day, while reading Psalm 90:12, Alex was struck by the phrase "teach us to number our days." It reminded him of the importance of valuing time and using it wisely. He realized that procrastination was robbing him of the opportunity to grow, learn, and achieve his goals.

Alex decided to implement practical strategies to overcome procrastination. He started by breaking tasks into smaller, manageable steps and creating a schedule with specific deadlines. He also learned to prioritize his time, focusing on the most important tasks first. By taking these proactive measures, Alex found that he was more productive, less stressed, and able to achieve better results.

The story of Alex teaches us the importance of managing procrastination in our academic journey. Procrastination hinders our growth, steals our time, and can lead to unnecessary stress. By embracing discipline, setting clear goals, and utilizing our time wisely, we can overcome the temptation to delay and achieve greater success.

Do you struggle with procrastination? What are some common triggers or excuses that lead you to delay tasks?

In what ways can you prioritize your time and focus on the most important tasks? How can you resist the temptation to engage in distractions and time-wasting activities?

How does the verse from Psalm 90:12 influence your perspective on managing procrastination? What does it mean to "number your days" and seek a heart of wisdom in the context of your academic journey?

Prayer:

Dear God,

Thank You for the gift of time and the opportunity to pursue education. Help me to recognize the temptation of procrastination and grant me the discipline to overcome it. Teach me to number my days, to value each moment, and to use my time wisely. Guide me in managing my tasks, setting clear goals, and resisting the distractions that lead to procrastination. May I grow in wisdom and achieve success as I prioritize diligence in my academic pursuits.

Amen.

11

---◄◊►---

OVERCOMING COMPARISON

____/____/_____

"For we are God's handiwork, created in Christ Jesus to do good works,
which God prepared in advance for us to do."

L et me share a story with you about Victor, a college student who
struggled with comparison and academic pressure. Throughout
his time in college, Victor found himself constantly comparing his
grades, achievements, and progress to those of his peers. He believed
that unless he achieved the same level of success as others, he was
somehow falling short.

One day, as Victor was seeking guidance and solace, he came across
Ephesians 2:10, which reminded him that he was God's handiwork,
created with unique gifts and a purpose. This verse shed light on the
truth that each person's academic journey is distinct and tailored to
their individual strengths and weaknesses.

The lesson Victor learned was that comparing himself to others was
a futile exercise that only led to feelings of inadequacy and discon-

tentment. He realized that his value and worth did not come from outperforming others, but from embracing his own unique path and fulfilling the purpose God had prepared for him.

From that moment on, Victor chose to shift his focus from comparison to self-discovery and growth. He acknowledged his strengths and weaknesses, understanding that his journey was not about being better than others, but about becoming the best version of himself. He pursued subjects and opportunities that aligned with his passions, leveraging his talents to make a meaningful impact.

Through embracing his unique path, Victor found a sense of fulfillment and joy in his academic pursuits. He understood that success should not be defined solely by external markers, but by his personal growth, character development, and the impact he had on others.

The lesson for us as college students is to overcome the pressure to compare ourselves to others and instead embrace our unique paths. We are each fearfully and wonderfully made, equipped with unique abilities and callings. Let us focus on cultivating our own talents, developing our skills, and making a difference in the world according to the plan God has for us.

Reflect on a time when you felt pressured to compare yourself to others academically. How did it affect your mindset and well-being? What lessons did you learn from that experience?

How does Ephesians 2:10 remind you of your worth and purpose? In what ways can you apply this truth to your academic journey?

How can you measure success in your academic journey beyond external achievements? Reflect on the impact you have on others, the growth of your character, and the fulfillment you find in pursuing your purpose.

Prayer:

Dear God,

Thank You for creating me as a unique individual with a purpose. Help me overcome the temptation to compare myself to others and instead embrace my own path in academics. Grant me the wisdom to identify and develop my strengths, while also acknowledging areas for growth. May my journey be guided by Your plan and bring glory to Your name.

Amen.

12

---◆○■---

SEEKING HELP AND SUPPORT

____ / ____ / _____

"For lack of guidance a nation falls, but victory is won through many advisers."

-PROVERBS 11:14

I f you don't already, try to recognize the importance of seeking help and support on your academic journey. It is not a sign of weakness but a wise choice. Utilize the resources available to you for academic success.

Proverbs 11:14 reminds us that victory comes from guidance and advice. Just as a nation falls without direction, trying to navigate your studies alone leads to unnecessary struggles. Seek support through tutoring services, study groups, and guidance from professors or mentors.

Tutoring services provide assistance in understanding complex subjects and clarifying doubts. Furthermore, it's a great idea to form study groups with classmates to exchange ideas and motivate each other, and also seek guidance from professors and mentors who can offer insights and direction.

Remember to seek emotional support from friends, family, and your faith community. We are designed to function in a community, learning from one another's experiences. Together, we can overcome obstacles and achieve academic success.

Have you hesitated to seek help? Reflect on any beliefs holding you back.

How can you utilize tutoring services or academic resources available to you?

Have you considered forming study groups? How can collaboration enhance your learning?

How comfortable are you in seeking guidance from professors or mentors?

Prayer:

Dear God,

Thank You for the resources and support available to me. Help me overcome hesitation and utilize these resources wisely. Grant me the wisdom to seek help, guidance, and encouragement. Surround me with a supportive community. May my pursuit of academic success align with Your plans.

Amen.

SOCIAL LIFE

13

---◄◄O►►---

IDENTITY AND PEER PRESSURE

____ / ____ / _____

"Do not conform to the pattern of this world, but be transformed by the renewing of your mind. Then you will be able to test and approve what God's will is—his good, pleasing and perfect will."

- ROMANS 12:2

N avigating social settings while staying true to yourself can be challenging. It's important to remember that your identity is rooted in Christ, not in the pressures or expectations of others. Let the Word of God guide you as you face peer pressure.

In Romans 12:2, we are encouraged not to conform to the pattern of this world but to be transformed by the renewing of our minds. Embrace the truth of who you are in Christ and allow His Word to shape your decisions and actions.

As you enter college, you may encounter situations where the desire to fit in or gain acceptance conflicts with your values. It's crucial to remember that compromising your beliefs to please others will never bring lasting fulfillment. Instead, focus on living out your faith authentically and seeking the approval of God, who loves you unconditionally.

Find strength in knowing that you are not alone. Surround yourself with like-minded friends who share your values and can support you in making choices that align with your identity in Christ. Seek fellowship in campus ministries or Christian organizations where you can grow spiritually and build meaningful connections.

When faced with peer pressure, pause and reflect on your values and the teachings of Scripture. Consider the consequences of your choices and how they align with your identity as a child of God. Choose to honor Him in all aspects of your life, including your social interactions.

Remember, staying true to yourself in social settings is not always easy, but it's worth it. It's an opportunity to be a light and a witness for Christ. By living in alignment with your faith, you can inspire and impact others, showing them the beauty of a life centered on Christ.

Have you ever felt pressured to compromise your values in social situations? How did you handle it?

In what ways can you actively cultivate and express your identity in Christ while navigating social settings?

Reflect on the verse from Romans 12:2. What does it mean to be transformed by the renewing of your mind?

Prayer:

Dear God,

Thank You for creating me with a unique identity and purpose. Help me stay true to myself in all social settings, even when faced with peer pressure. Renew my mind with Your Word and guide me in making choices that align with Your will. Surround me with friends who share my values and inspire me to grow in faith. May my life reflect Your love and truth.

Amen.

14

PEER INFLUENCE AND ACCOUNTABILITY

___/___/_____

"Do not be misled: 'Bad company corrupts good character.'"

- 1 CORINTHIANS 15:33

A llow me to share a story that illustrates the power of peer influence and the importance of surrounding yourself with positive role models. A young man named Elijah entered college with great aspirations. However, he quickly fell into the wrong crowd, seeking acceptance and validation in all the wrong places.

Elijah's newfound friends led him down a destructive path, indulging in excessive partying, substance abuse, and reckless behavior. The negative influence began to take its toll, affecting his academic performance, relationships, and overall well-being. Elijah's character started to change, and he found himself spiraling into a life he never intended to lead.

One day, Elijah met Nathan, a fellow college student who radiated positivity, integrity, and purpose. Nathan exemplified the qualities Elijah aspired to possess. Intrigued by Nathan's strong character, Elijah took the courageous step of distancing himself from his negative influences and seeking the company of positive role models.

Through his friendship with Nathan, Elijah began to rebuild his life. He found support, encouragement, and accountability. Nathan introduced him to a community of like-minded individuals who inspired personal growth, academic excellence, and a deepened faith. Elijah's grades improved, he rediscovered his passion for his chosen field of study, and he surrounded himself with friends who uplifted him.

The lesson from Elijah's story is clear: the company we keep can profoundly impact our lives. Negative influences can lead us astray, compromising our character and hindering our growth. Conversely, positive role models can inspire us, uplift us, and help us become the best versions of ourselves.

As you navigate college, seek out positive role models who align with your values and aspirations. Surround yourself with friends who support and encourage your personal and spiritual growth. Engage in campus organizations, clubs, or faith-based groups that foster a community of accountability and positive influence.

Remember the words of 1 Corinthians 15:33, "Do not be misled: 'Bad company corrupts good character.'" Choose your company wisely, for it has the power to shape your character and influence your future.

Have you ever experienced the negative influence of peer pressure? How did it affect your character and choices?

Are there any relationships or friendships that are negatively impacting your college experience? How can you take steps to distance yourself from those influences?

Reflect on the positive role models in your life. How have they influenced you and contributed to your personal growth?

Prayer:

Dear God,

Thank You for guiding us and placing positive role models in our lives. Help us to recognize the power of peer influence and to seek accountability through healthy relationships. Grant us the wisdom and discernment to surround ourselves with positive influences that align with our values and aspirations. Strengthen us to be positive role models for others, shining Your light in the world.

Amen.

———◆◇◆———

15

BUILDING MEANINGFUL
FRIENDSHIPS

____ / ____ / _____

"A friend loves at all times, and a brother is born for a time of adversity."

- PROVERBS 17:17

A s you navigate your social life in college, one of the most rewarding aspects is building meaningful friendships. These friendships can shape your college experience, provide support during challenging times, and contribute to your personal growth and spiritual development. Let us explore together the importance of cultivating authentic connections.

Proverbs 17:17 reminds us that a friend loves at all times and is there for us in times of adversity. This verse highlights the significance of true friendship and the impact it can have on our lives. As you embark on this journey, consider the following insights.

Firstly, be intentional about seeking like-minded individuals who share your values and faith. Surrounding yourself with friends who align with your beliefs and aspirations creates a supportive community that encourages personal and spiritual growth. Seek out Christian organizations, campus ministries, or clubs that resonate with your interests and values. These communities can provide opportunities to connect with individuals who share similar convictions and foster authentic friendships.

Secondly, be open and vulnerable in your interactions. Genuine connections are built on trust, honesty, and mutual understanding. Share your thoughts, experiences, and struggles with others, and be receptive to listening and supporting them in return. Authenticity creates a foundation for meaningful relationships and fosters a sense of belonging within a community.

Taking ownership of your social life means actively investing in building friendships that align with your values and aspirations. It requires effort, vulnerability, and a willingness to prioritize quality over quantity. Remember that meaningful friendships take time to cultivate, and not every connection will become deep and lasting. Be patient, be yourself, and trust that God will guide you to the right people.

Reflect on the verse from Proverbs 17:17. What qualities do you value in a friend, and how can you embody those qualities in your own relationships?

Have you experienced the impact of a meaningful friendship in your life? How did it shape you and contribute to your personal growth?

What steps can you take to find like-minded individuals and cultivate authentic connections on your college campus?

Prayer:

Dear God,

Thank You for the gift of friendship and the potential it holds for personal growth and spiritual development. Guide me in seeking like-minded individuals who share my values and aspirations. Grant me the wisdom to cultivate authentic connections and the courage to be vulnerable and genuine in my interactions. May the friendships I build bring glory to Your name and enrich my college experience.

Amen.

16

OVERCOMING LONELINESS

_____ / _____ / _____

"Let us think of ways to motivate one another to acts of love and good works. And let us not neglect our meeting together, as some people do, but encourage one another."

- HEBREWS 10:24-25

Loneliness can be a challenging aspect of the college experience, but it doesn't have to define your journey. The key to overcoming loneliness lies in finding connection and community.

In Hebrews 10:24-25, we are encouraged to motivate one another and gather together. These verses highlight the power of community in supporting and uplifting us during times of isolation.

To combat loneliness, take ownership of your social life by engaging in campus activities and organizations that align with your interests. Through these groups, you can meet like-minded individuals and forge meaningful connections.

Don't be afraid to reach out and connect with others. Attend events, strike up conversations, and be open to meeting new people. Taking small steps outside your comfort zone can lead to valuable friendships and a sense of belonging.

By embracing community, you not only overcome loneliness but also create a network of support and encouragement. Together, you can inspire one another to acts of love and good works, finding fulfillment and joy in genuine friendships.

Reflect on a time when you felt lonely during college. How did it affect you, and what steps can you take to prevent or overcome loneliness?

What specific campus activities or organizations align with your interests? How can you get involved?

What fears or hesitations do you have in reaching out to others? How can you overcome them?

Share an experience when you took the initiative to connect with someone. How did it impact your college experience?

Prayer:

Dear God,

Help me find connection and community during my college journey. Give me the courage to engage in activities and reach out to others. Guide me to like-minded individuals who will support and uplift me. May my friendships inspire acts of love and good works, bringing joy and fulfillment to my life.

Amen.

17

——◆◇◆——

FOSTERING INCLUSIVITY

____ / ____ / _____

"Accept one another, then, just as Christ accepted you, in order to bring praise to God."

- ROMANS 15:7

I n the diverse tapestry of college life, fostering inclusivity is crucial in creating an environment of belonging and acceptance. By embracing diversity, challenging biases, and extending love and acceptance to all, we can cultivate a community that reflects the heart of Christ.

In Romans 15:7, we are called to accept one another, just as Christ accepted us. This verse reminds us that our acceptance of others brings praise to God. It emphasizes the importance of recognizing the inherent worth and value of every individual, regardless of their background or differences.

As you journey through college, take ownership of your education by actively fostering inclusivity. Challenge your own biases and preconceptions, seeking to understand and appreciate the unique perspectives and experiences of those around you.

Extend kindness and acceptance to everyone you encounter, regardless of their race, ethnicity, gender, socioeconomic status, or beliefs. Be intentional in building relationships and creating spaces where everyone feels welcome, valued, and heard.

Embrace opportunities to engage in meaningful conversations about diversity and inclusion. Participate in events, workshops, and discussions that promote understanding, empathy, and unity. By actively seeking to learn from others and valuing their experiences, you contribute to a richer and more inclusive college experience for all.

Remember that small acts of kindness and inclusion can have a profound impact on individuals' lives. Even a simple gesture of reaching out to someone who may feel marginalized or overlooked can make a significant difference. Your commitment to fostering inclusivity creates ripples of love, acceptance, and belonging within your college community.

Reflect on a time when you witnessed or experienced exclusion or discrimination. How did it make you feel, and what can you do differently to promote inclusivity?

How does the verse from Romans 15:7 inspire you to embrace diversity and extend acceptance to others?

What biases or stereotypes do you need to confront and challenge within yourself? How can you actively work towards dismantling them? -

Prayer:

Dear God,

Thank you for the diversity of our college community. Help me to actively foster inclusivity, challenge biases, and extend love and acceptance to all. Grant me the courage to reach out to others, embrace differences, and create a welcoming environment. May my actions bring praise to Your name and reflect the heart of Christ.

Amen.

18

SOCIAL MEDIA AND ONLINE PRESENCE

____ / ____ / _____

"Do not conform to the pattern of this world, but be transformed by the renewing of your mind."

- ROMANS 12:2

I n today's digital age, social media plays a significant role in our lives. It connects us, entertains us, and keeps us informed. However, it's essential to navigate the digital world with wisdom and discernment, ensuring that our online presence aligns with our values and promotes a healthy mindset.

I remember when I was in college, social media had just started gaining popularity. It was an exciting and powerful tool, but it also brought challenges. I witnessed how easy it was to get caught up in the allure of likes, followers, and comparison.

One day, a close friend of mine, Jake, confided in me about his struggles with social media. He felt constant pressure to portray an idealized version of himself, and the pursuit of validation through likes and comments consumed him. It affected his self-worth and left him feeling empty.

Together, we explored the importance of being true to oneself in the digital world. We delved into Romans 12:2, which urges us not to conform to the pattern of this world but to be transformed by the renewing of our minds.

We learned that managing our online presence requires authenticity and intentionality. Instead of seeking validation from others, we should focus on being genuine, sharing our joys, struggles, and aspirations without fear of judgment. By doing so, we create an environment where others feel safe to do the same.

We also realized the significance of balancing our time spent on social media. We developed healthy habits, setting boundaries and taking breaks when we felt overwhelmed. We discovered that engaging in real-life connections and experiences was essential for our personal growth and well-being.

How does your online presence reflect your values and character? Are there any changes you need to make?

In what ways has social media influenced your perception of self-worth? How can you prioritize your true identity in Christ over external validation?

Have you ever felt the pressure to conform or compare yourself to others on social media? How did it impact your mindset and emotions?

What boundaries can you set to manage your time and energy spent on social media? How can you ensure a healthy balance between online engagement and real-life connections?

How can you use your online presence as an opportunity to positively impact others?

Prayer:

Dear God,

Thank You for the gift of technology and the digital world. Guide me in using social media responsibly and with discernment. Help me to be authentic and intentional in my online presence, reflecting Your love and grace. Grant me the wisdom to manage my time and energy wisely, finding a healthy balance between the digital realm and real-life connections.

Amen.

19

CONFLICT RESOLUTION

_____ / _____ / _____

"If it is possible, as far as it depends on you, live at peace with everyone."

- ROMANS 12:18

Conflicts are an inevitable part of life, and college is no exception. I remember a time during my college years when I found myself in the midst of a heated disagreement with a close friend. Our different viewpoints clashed, and tension grew. It felt like our relationship was on the verge of crumbling.

In that moment, I realized the importance of taking ownership of conflicts and seeking resolution. I took a step back and decided to approach the situation with humility and a genuine desire to understand my friend's perspective. Instead of arguing or trying to prove my point, I chose to listen attentively and empathize with their feelings.

Through open communication and a willingness to find common ground, we were able to work through our differences. We discovered that our friendship was worth more than being right. We learned the power of forgiveness and reconciliation, as we both acknowledged our mistakes and extended grace to one another.

From that experience, I understood that conflict resolution requires effort and a commitment to restoring relationships. It's about actively pursuing peace and understanding, even when it's difficult. By taking ownership of conflicts, seeking open communication, and practicing forgiveness, we can rebuild and strengthen our relationships.

Can you recall a time when you experienced a conflict with a friend or peer? How did you initially respond, and what did you learn from that experience?

Reflect on the verse from Romans 12:18. How can you apply its wisdom to conflict resolution and restoring relationships in your own life?

Think about a current or past conflict. How can you take ownership of the situation and initiate a conversation for resolution? What steps can you take to cultivate forgiveness and reconciliation?

Share a time when you successfully resolved a conflict and restored a relationship. How did that experience shape your understanding of conflict resolution?

Prayer:

Dear God,

Thank you for guiding us in resolving conflicts and restoring relationships. Teach us to approach disagreements with humility, empathy, and a commitment to understanding one another. Grant us the strength and wisdom to actively pursue peace and reconciliation. May our interactions be marked by grace, forgiveness, and a genuine desire to restore broken connections.

Amen.

20

RESPECTING BOUNDARIES

___ / ___ / _____

"Above all else, guard your heart, for everything you do flows from it."

– PROVERBS 4:23

During my college years, I learned a valuable lesson about the importance of respecting boundaries—both in honoring others' boundaries and setting personal boundaries. It's crucial to navigate relationships and social interactions with respect, sensitivity, and a clear understanding of consent.

In Proverbs 4:23, we are reminded to guard our hearts because everything we do flows from it. This verse speaks to the significance of maintaining healthy boundaries to protect ourselves and others. Respecting boundaries is not only an act of kindness but also an expression of love and consideration for others' well-being.

Understanding consent is an essential aspect of respecting boundaries. Consent should be enthusiastic, clear, and freely given. It is important to seek explicit consent in all aspects of relationships, whether it's physical intimacy, sharing personal information, or engaging in social activities. Consent should never be assumed or coerced but rather communicated and respected at all times.

Setting personal boundaries is equally important. It means recognizing your limits, values, and needs, and communicating them assertively and respectfully. Setting boundaries empowers you to take ownership of your own well-being and ensures that your relationships are built on mutual respect and understanding.

Taking ownership of your education goes beyond academic pursuits—it extends to your personal growth, relationships, and interactions. By being intentional about respecting boundaries, you create a safe and healthy environment for yourself and those around you. It allows you to build genuine connections and contribute positively to the community.

Reflect on a time when you felt your boundaries were crossed or when you unintentionally crossed someone else's boundaries. How did it impact you or the other person? What did you learn from that experience?

Consider the verse from Proverbs 4:23. How can guarding your heart by respecting boundaries contribute to your overall well-being and growth?

How can you actively practice and promote consent in your relationships and social interactions?

Prayer:

Dear God,

Thank you for teaching us the importance of respecting boundaries. Help us to navigate relationships and social interactions with respect, sensitivity, and understanding. Grant us the wisdom to set healthy boundaries and honor the boundaries of others. May our actions be rooted in love and contribute to a community built on mutual respect and care.

Amen.

FINANCIAL MANAGEMENT

———◆○◆———

21

STEWARDSHIP

____ / ____ / _____

"Yours, Lord, is the greatness and the power and the glory and the majesty and the splendor, for everything in heaven and earth is yours. Yours, Lord, is the kingdom; you are exalted as head over all."

- 1 CHRONICLES 29:11 (NIV)

Mark was a devoted Christian who understood the importance of stewardship in his life. He had just started his freshman year, and as he settled into his dorm room, he reflected on the verse from 1 Chronicles 29:11. Mark realized that everything he had, including his education, talents, and financial resources, was a gift from God. He understood that he was merely a steward of these blessings, entrusted with the responsibility to use them wisely for God's purposes.

As the semester progressed, Mark noticed that many of his friends were spending their money recklessly. They were caught up in the excitement of newfound independence and the desire to fit in. However, Mark felt a conviction to approach his finances differently. He prayed for wisdom and sought guidance from older Christian mentors who had walked the college journey before him.

Mark learned valuable lessons about financial management. He embraced the concept of stewardship, recognizing that every dollar he spent was a decision that could either align with God's purposes or veer him off track. He started budgeting his expenses, distinguishing between needs and wants. Mark discovered the joy of saving money and practiced disciplined spending habits.

In the midst of his college experience, Mark realized that stewardship went beyond finances. It extended to his time, talents, and relationships as well. He became intentional about managing his time wisely, prioritizing his studies, involvement in campus activities, and nurturing meaningful friendships. Mark also recognized that his God-given talents were meant to be used for serving others and bringing glory to God.

How can you apply the concept of stewardship to your finances as a college student?

What are some practical steps you can take to manage your money wisely and align your spending with God's purposes?

How can practicing stewardship bring joy and fulfillment to your college journey?

Prayer:

Dear God,

Thank You for the reminder that everything we have is ultimately Yours. Help us to embrace the concept of stewardship and recognize our responsibility in managing our finances, time, talents, and relationships for Your purposes. Grant us wisdom and discipline as we navigate the college journey, making choices that align with Your will. May our lives be a testament to Your goodness and grace.

Amen.

22

⬤─◆─◇─◆─⬤

BUDGETING BASICS

____ / ____ / _____

"The plans of the diligent lead to profit as surely as haste leads to poverty."

- PROVERBS 21:5

I n the realm of personal finance, one crucial skill that can greatly impact your college journey and beyond is budgeting. Budgeting allows you to take control of your finances, make informed decisions, and work towards your financial goals. Let's explore the importance of budgeting and the practical steps you can take to create and manage a college budget.

Budgeting is a powerful tool that helps you understand where your money is coming from and where it's going. It enables you to allocate your financial resources wisely, distinguishing between needs and wants, and ensuring that your spending aligns with your priorities. By creating a budget, you gain clarity and take ownership of your financial situation.

To start budgeting effectively, begin by tracking your income and expenses. List all your sources of income, such as scholarships, part-time jobs, or allowances, and identify your fixed expenses like tuition, rent, and utilities. Consider your variable expenses, including groceries, transportation, entertainment, and other miscellaneous costs. This exercise will help you understand your cash flow and identify areas where you can save or make adjustments.

With a clear understanding of your finances, set specific financial goals. Whether it's saving for emergencies, paying off student loans, or investing in your future, having goals provides direction and motivation. Break down your goals into achievable steps and incorporate them into your budget. Prioritize your spending to align with your goals and be intentional about saving for the future.

As you embark on your budgeting journey, remember the wisdom of Proverbs 21:5. Diligent planning and thoughtful financial management lead to profit and financial well-being. By approaching your finances with discipline and careful consideration, you can avoid unnecessary debt, reduce financial stress, and build a solid foundation for your future.

Budgeting is not merely a practical exercise but also an act of stewardship. Recognize that all you have is a gift from God, and by managing your finances wisely, you honor Him. Consider how you can use your financial resources to bless others and make a positive impact. By budgeting responsibly, you can develop lifelong habits that reflect your commitment to stewardship and gratitude.

Reflect on your current financial habits and take proactive steps to create and manage a college budget. Embrace the principles of discipline, intentionality, and stewardship as you navigate the realm of personal finance. Let your budgeting journey be a testament to your desire to be a responsible steward of the resources entrusted to you.

How would creating and managing a budget contribute to your college journey and financial well-being?

Take a moment to assess your current financial situation. Are you tracking your income and expenses? What adjustments can you make to align your spending with your priorities and goals?

Reflect on Proverbs 21:5. What does it mean to plan diligently in the context of personal finance? How can you apply this principle to your budgeting practice?

Prayer:

Dear God,

Thank you for the resources you have provided us, including our finances. Guide us as we embark on the journey of creating and managing a college budget. Help us exercise discipline, wisdom, and stewardship in our financial decisions. May our budgeting efforts reflect our desire to honor you and use our resources for your glory.

Amen.

23

AVOIDING DEBT

____ / ____ / _____

"The borrower is slave to the lender."

- PROVERBS 22:7

L et me share a valuable lesson about avoiding debt that I learned during my college years. John, my fellow student, took out multiple loans to fund his extravagant lifestyle. He was enticed by credit card offers, unaware of the long-term consequences. Graduation approached, and reality hit him hard as he faced a mountain of debt and limited job prospects.

This story reminds us of the importance of making wise choices to minimize financial burdens. Debt can quickly become a heavy burden that restricts your freedom and limits your options. Here are key insights to consider:

1. Live within your means: Embrace a lifestyle that aligns with your financial reality. Prioritize needs over wants and avoid unnecessary expenses that can lead to debt accumulation.

2. Develop a budget: Create a realistic budget that accounts for your income and expenses. Be intentional about saving and allocate funds towards debt repayment, ensuring you stay on track and avoid falling into the debt trap.

3. Seek alternatives to debt: Explore scholarships, grants, part-time work, and other avenues to fund your education and cover expenses. Minimize your reliance on loans by maximizing available resources.

4. Exercise financial discipline: Learn to distinguish between essential and non-essential purchases. Develop the habit of saving and resist the temptation of impulsive spending. Remember, every financial decision has long-term consequences.

Reflecting on Proverbs 22:7, we are reminded that borrowing can lead to a loss of freedom. Let us be wise stewards of the resources God has entrusted us with, avoiding unnecessary debt and embracing financial freedom.

How has this devotion challenged your perspective on debt and financial responsibility? Are there any changes you feel prompted to make in your approach to managing money?

Reflect on your current financial habits and spending patterns. Are there areas where you could make adjustments to avoid unnecessary debt? What steps can you take to live within your means and prioritize financial stability?

Consider your long-term financial goals. How does the idea of avoiding debt align with your aspirations? What strategies can you implement to minimize financial burdens and stay on track towards your goals?

Prayer:

Dear God,

Grant us wisdom and discipline as we navigate our finances. Help us make wise choices, avoid unnecessary debt, and honor you with our financial decisions. May we find freedom and peace by living within our means and relying on your provision.

Amen.

24

---◆◇◆---

PART-TIME JOBS AND FINANCIAL RESPONSIBILITY

___ / ___ / _____

"Do you see someone skilled in their work? They will serve before kings;
they will not serve before officials of low rank."

- PROVERBS 22:29 (NIV)

D ear college student, I want to share with you the importance of balancing your part-time job, studies, and financial responsibilities. As someone who has been through college, I understand the challenges you may face in managing your time and finances. It can be tempting to prioritize work solely for financial gain, but it's crucial to remember that education is an investment in your future.

Finding the right balance between work and studies is key. While a part-time job can provide financial support and valuable work experience, it should never overshadow your primary purpose of being a student. Your education is an opportunity for growth, knowledge, and preparing for the future. Take ownership of your education by prioritizing your studies and using your part-time job as a means to support your goals rather than hinder them.

Consider your time management skills and create a schedule that allows you to allocate dedicated time for both work and studies. Be mindful of your limitations and avoid overcommitting yourself, as burnout can negatively impact your academic performance. Seek guidance from mentors or advisors who can help you navigate the balance between work and

How have you been managing the balance between your part-time job and studies? Are there any adjustments you need to make to find a healthier balance?

What are your long-term goals and aspirations? How does your part-time job align with those goals, and how can you ensure it supports your educational journey?

Are there any areas where you struggle to find balance or prioritize your studies? How can you seek support or implement strategies to overcome these challenges?

Prayer:

Dear God,

Grant us wisdom and discernment as we navigate the demands of work, studies, and financial responsibilities. Help us find balance and prioritize our education while making the most of our part-time jobs. Guide us in using our time and resources wisely, so that we may grow in knowledge and honor You in all that we do.

Amen.

———◄◄○►►———

25

SAVING FOR THE FUTURE

___ / ___ / _____

"The wise store up choice food and olive oil, but fools gulp theirs down."

-PROVERBS 21:20 (NIV)

W e've all been tempted by the allure of instant gratification and spending every dollar as soon as it comes in. However, I want to encourage you to think long-term and develop a mindset of saving for your future.

Establishing a habit of saving is not only about accumulating wealth but also about preparing for the uncertainties and opportunities that lie ahead. It requires discipline, sacrifice, and delayed gratification. By saving, you create a safety net for emergencies and unexpected expenses. Additionally, saving for your post-graduation plans, whether it's further education, starting a business, or traveling, allows you to pursue your dreams without the burden of excessive debt.

Taking ownership of your education means recognizing that financial responsibility is a part of the journey. It means being intentional about budgeting, tracking expenses, and setting aside a portion of your income for savings. Start small, even if it's just a few dollars each month, and gradually increase your savings as you are able to. Embrace the mindset that every dollar saved is an investment in your future and a demonstration of good stewardship.

What are your long-term goals and aspirations? How can saving money now contribute to their achievement?

How can you prioritize saving in your current financial situation? Are there any areas of unnecessary spending that you can identify and cut back on?

What are some practical steps you can take to establish good financial habits, such as creating a budget, automating savings, or seeking advice from a financial advisor or mentor?

Prayer:

Dear God,

We seek Your guidance and wisdom in our financial management. Help us develop disciplined habits of saving and stewardship, knowing that our future is in Your hands. Give us the strength to resist the allure of immediate gratification and the courage to make wise financial decisions. May our actions today reflect our trust in Your provision and our commitment to responsible stewardship.

Amen.

26

PRACTICING CONTENTMENT

____ / ____ / _____

"The wise store up choice food and olive oil, but fools gulp theirs down."

- PROVERBS 21:20 (NIV)

I magine a college student named Noah who had just started their journey at a university. Like many students, Noah was excited about the newfound freedom and opportunities that college life offered. With a part-time job and a growing social circle, it seemed like the perfect time to enjoy life to the fullest. However, amidst the excitement, Noah had a realization: the importance of saving for the future.

One day, Noah's friend, Marcus, shared a story about his older brother who had graduated a few years ago. Despite landing a well-paying job, Marcus's brother found himself burdened by student loan repayments and other financial obligations. He confessed that he wished he had developed better saving habits during his college years. Inspired by this story, Noah began to reflect on their own financial situation.

Taking a step back, Noah realized that saving money wasn't just about restriction or missing out on present enjoyment. It was about being prepared for the future and having the freedom to pursue long-term goals. The story of Marcus's brother became a wake-up call for Noah, highlighting the importance of establishing good financial habits early on.

In that moment, Noah made a commitment to take ownership of their education, not just academically, but also financially. They started by creating a budget and identifying areas where unnecessary expenses could be reduced. With each paycheck, a portion was diligently set aside for savings. It wasn't always easy, as temptations to splurge on immediate desires arose. However, the vision of a secure and financially independent future fueled Noah's determination.

Through the story of Noah's journey, we can learn the valuable lesson of saving for the future. It's not about depriving ourselves of present enjoyment, but rather about making intentional choices that align with our long-term goals. By taking ownership of our education, we recognize the importance of financial responsibility and develop the discipline to save and invest wisely.

How can you develop good saving habits while in college, even when faced with temptations to spend impulsively?

What are some strategies you can implement to stay motivated and disciplined in your saving efforts?

How can taking ownership of your financial education positively impact your overall college experience and set you up for future success?

Prayer:

Dear God,

We thank You for the wisdom and insight to recognize the importance of saving for the future. Help us, like Noah, to take ownership of our financial responsibilities and develop disciplined saving habits. Grant us the strength to resist the temptations of immediate desires and focus on the long-term goals You have for us. Guide us in making wise financial decisions throughout our college journey and beyond.

Amen.

YOUR SPIRITUAL LIFE

27

PRIORITIZING PERSONAL DEVOTIONS

___ / ___ / _____

"You, God, are my God, earnestly I seek you; I thirst for you, my whole being longs for you, in a dry and parched land where there is no water."

- PSALM 63:1 (NIV)

As a college student, I vividly remember the demands and busyness that surrounded me. Balancing classes, assignments, social activities, and part-time jobs seemed overwhelming at times. In the midst of it all, I discovered the importance of prioritizing personal devotions and cultivating a consistent quiet time with God.

There was a season when I neglected my spiritual life, allowing the busyness to consume my days. I felt spiritually parched, longing for the refreshing presence of God. It was during that time that I stumbled upon Psalm 63:1, where David passionately expressed his thirst for God. His words resonated with me, and I realized that I, too, longed for a deep and intimate relationship with Him.

I made a conscious decision to take ownership of my spiritual education. I started by setting aside a specific time each day for personal devotions. Whether it was early mornings or late nights, I carved out moments to seek God, read His Word, and spend time in prayer. It wasn't always easy to remain consistent, but I discovered that the discipline and effort invested in my personal devotional routine yielded immeasurable rewards.

Through this journey, I learned that prioritizing personal devotions was not just another task on my to-do list. It was a lifeline, a source of strength, wisdom, and guidance amidst the challenges of college life. Cultivating a consistent quiet time allowed me to nurture my relationship with God and discover His faithfulness in every aspect of my life.

What are some practical steps you can take to prioritize personal devotions in your college routine? How can you create a consistent quiet time for seeking God?

Reflect on a time when you felt spiritually dry or distant from God. What factors contributed to that situation, and how could a consistent devotional routine have made a difference?

How has God revealed His faithfulness and wisdom to you through personal devotions? Share a specific moment when spending time with Him brought clarity, comfort, or guidance in your college journey.

Prayer:

Dear God,

We thank You for the gift of personal devotions and the opportunity to seek You in quiet moments. Help us prioritize time with You amidst the busyness of college life. Grant us discipline and wisdom as we cultivate a consistent devotional routine. As we seek You, may You reveal Yourself to us in powerful ways and strengthen our faith.

Amen.

28

FINDING COMMUNITY

___ / ___ / _____

"Let us not give up meeting together, as some are in the habit of doing, but let us encourage one another—and all the more as you see the Day approaching."

- HEBREWS 10:25 (NIV)

D uring my college years, I realized the value of finding and engaging in Christian community. It was in the midst of lectures, dorm rooms, and campus activities that I longed for genuine connections with believers who could support, encourage, and spur me on in my faith.

In the pursuit of such a community, I encountered like-minded individuals who shared a passion for Christ. We formed a small group where we could freely worship, pray, and study the Bible together. These gatherings became a haven, a place where we could be vulnerable and grow spiritually. We held each other accountable, offering guidance and support in our shared journey of faith.

Hebrews 10:25 emphasizes the importance of not giving up meeting together. As the author reminds us, meeting in community is not merely a suggestion but a vital part of our Christian walk. It is through these connections that we find encouragement, inspiration, and the opportunity to grow in our relationship with God.

Finding community in college may require effort and stepping out of your comfort zone. It might involve joining a campus ministry, participating in Bible study groups, or seeking out fellowship opportunities in local churches. But the rewards are immeasurable. In Christian community, you will discover lasting friendships, find mentors to guide you, and experience the power of united worship.

How have you experienced the benefits of Christian community in your college journey? Share a specific instance where the support and encouragement of fellow believers made a difference in your spiritual growth.

Reflect on the challenges you face in finding or engaging in Christian community. What steps can you take to overcome these obstacles and actively seek genuine connections with other believers?

How can you contribute to the growth and well-being of the Christian community around you? In what ways can you be an encouragement and source of support for others in their faith journey?

Prayer:

Dear God,

Let us recognize the importance of Christian community. Guide us in finding like-minded believers who can support, encourage, and inspire us in our faith. Help us overcome any barriers and fears that hinder us from actively engaging in community. May we be a source of encouragement and love to those around us, building genuine connections that glorify You.

In Jesus' name, we pray. Amen.

29

———◀O▶———

CULTIVATING A SPIRIT OF GRATITUDE

_____ / _____ / _____

"Give thanks in all circumstances; for this is God's will for you in Christ Jesus."

-1 THESSALONIANS 5:18 (NIV)

In your college years, you will encounter seasons of both joy and difficulty. There will be moments of triumph, academic successes, and cherished friendships. But there will also be times of stress, disappointments, and uncertainty about the future. In the midst of it all, it is important to cultivate a spirit of gratitude and find joy in every season.

I remember a particular season that stands out in my memory. I faced overwhelming academic pressure, struggling to balance my coursework and extracurricular commitments. It felt as if the weight of the world was on my shoulders, and joy seemed elusive. In the midst of my distress, I stumbled upon 1 Thessalonians 5:18, which urged me to give thanks in all circumstances.

I realized that gratitude was not dependent on my circumstances but on my perspective. I began intentionally seeking out moments of thanksgiving, no matter how small. I thanked God for the knowledge I gained through my studies, for the opportunity to learn and grow, and for the support and encouragement of friends and family. As I shifted my focus from my challenges to God's blessings, my perspective shifted, and a spirit of gratitude permeated my college experience.

The lesson I learned was profound, and it is one that applies to you as well. Gratitude has the power to transform your heart and mind. It shifts your focus from what you lack to what you have, from complaints to thanksgiving. In every season of your college life, whether joyful or challenging, there are reasons to be grateful. Cultivating a spirit of gratitude will allow you to find joy, peace, and contentment amidst the ups and downs.

How can you cultivate a spirit of gratitude in your college journey? Take a moment to reflect on the blessings and provisions of God in your life. How can you express thanksgiving in both the big and small moments?

In difficult seasons, how can gratitude help you find joy and peace? Share a specific challenge you are currently facing and think of ways you can choose gratitude and shift your perspective towards God's faithfulness.

Consider the impact of a grateful heart on your relationships with others. How can expressing gratitude to your friends, family, and mentors contribute to building stronger connections and fostering a positive atmosphere?

Prayer:

Dear God,

Teach us to cultivate a spirit of gratitude in every season of our college journey. Help us to recognize Your blessings, even in difficult circumstances. Fill our hearts with joy and contentment as we shift our perspective from complaints to thanksgiving. May our lives be a testimony of Your faithfulness and goodness.

Amen.

30

INTEGRATING FAITH AND LEARNING

___/ ___/ _____

"Whatever you do, work at it with all your heart, as working for the Lord, not for human masters."

- COLOSSIANS 3:23 (NIV)

In your college years, you will discover the beauty of integrating faith and learning. As you engage in your academic pursuits, you will realize that every subject and discipline has the potential to deepen your understanding of God's creation and His truth. Let me share a story of a turning point in my own journey of connecting academics with biblical truths.

I was enrolled in a philosophy course, where we explored profound questions about the meaning of life, ethics, and existence. At first, I approached the subject purely from an intellectual standpoint, eager to grasp complex theories and philosophies. However, as I delved deeper into the course material, I realized the relevance of connecting these philosophical ideas with my faith.

Colossians 3:23 reminded me that whatever we do, including our academic pursuits, should be done wholeheartedly as an offering to God. It was a revelation for me. I began to view my philosophy studies as an opportunity to seek truth, to discern God's wisdom even in the midst of contrasting worldviews. It challenged me to critically engage with the ideas presented, filtering them through the lens of biblical truth.

Through this process, I discovered that faith and learning were not separate compartments but intertwined aspects of my life. I could explore various academic disciplines, recognizing that each subject held glimpses of God's handiwork. The integration of faith and learning allowed me to approach my studies with purpose, to seek wisdom that would shape my worldview and deepen my relationship with God.

The lesson I learned was profound, and it is one that applies to you as well. Your academic pursuits can be avenues to grow in your understanding of God and His truth. When you approach your studies with an open heart and a desire to connect them with biblical principles, you unlock the potential for transformation and deeper insight.

How can you integrate your faith and learning in your college journey? Reflect on your academic pursuits and identify areas where you can seek connections with biblical truths. How can your studies contribute to your spiritual growth?

In what ways can you approach your studies as an offering to God? How does the perspective of working for the Lord rather than human masters shape your attitude and approach to learning?

Consider a specific subject or discipline you are currently studying. How can you explore its connection to your faith? Are there biblical principles or teachings that can shed light on the topics you are encountering?

Prayer:

Dear God,

Help us integrate our faith and learning in our college journey. Open our hearts and minds to recognize Your truth in every subject and discipline. May our studies be opportunities to seek wisdom, discern truth, and grow in our understanding of Your creation. Guide us as we approach our academic pursuits as offerings to You. May our knowledge and insights deepen our relationship with You and equip us to impact the world for Your glory.

Amen.

———◆◇◆———

31

OVERCOMING SPIRITUAL DRYNESS

___ / ___ / _____

"As the deer pants for streams of water, so my soul pants for you, my God. My soul thirsts for God, for the living God."

- PSALM 42:1-2

I magine this: You're in the middle of a scorching desert, feeling parched and exhausted. Your soul longs for refreshment, for a deep connection with God. In college, it's not uncommon to experience seasons of spiritual dryness—times when your faith feels distant, when it seems challenging to find that spark of intimacy with God.

Let me assure you, dear college student, that experiencing spiritual dryness is a normal part of the journey. It doesn't mean your faith is failing or that God has abandoned you. It's a reminder that your soul, just like a deer searching for water, yearns for a vibrant relationship with God.

During your college years, you may encounter moments when the demands of academics, relationships, and personal struggles leave little room for nurturing your spiritual life. But don't lose heart. Instead, take intentional steps to rekindle your connection with God.

Start by creating space in your busy schedule for prayer, Bible reading, and reflection. Seek out like-minded believers who can provide support and encouragement along the way. Engage in worship, whether through personal devotion or joining a Christian community. Remember, even small moments of spiritual investment can make a significant impact.

Have you ever experienced spiritual dryness? How did it feel, and what steps did you take to overcome it?

What are some practical ways you can create space for nurturing your relationship with God in the midst of college life?

How can you seek out support and encouragement from fellow believers to help you navigate spiritual dryness?

Prayer:

Dear God,

We acknowledge that spiritual dryness is a common experience in our college years. We ask for Your guidance and strength as we seek to nurture a vibrant relationship with You. Fill our souls with a deep longing for Your presence, and help us find the time and space to draw near to You. Refresh us, O God, and renew our spirits as we journey through college.

Amen.

32

THE POWER OF PRAYER

____ / ____ / _____

"Do not be anxious about anything, but in every situation, by prayer and petition, with thanksgiving, present your requests to God. And the peace of God, which transcends all understanding, will guard your hearts and your minds in Christ Jesus."

- PHILIPPIANS 4:6-7

College life can be filled with various challenges, uncertainties, and moments of need. When you face difficult exams, relationship struggles, or decisions that leave you overwhelmed, remember the power of prayer.

Prayer is a powerful tool that allows you to draw near to God, seek His wisdom, find comfort, and receive guidance. It's a way to present your worries, concerns, and requests before the One who holds all things in His hands. God invites you to approach Him with a grateful heart, trusting that He hears your prayers and will provide the peace that surpasses all understanding.

In times of need, turn to prayer as a source of strength and hope. Pour out your heart to God, express gratitude for His faithfulness, and seek His direction. Remember that prayer is a two-way conversation, where you can listen for God's voice and discern His will.

How can you prioritize prayer in your college life, even amidst a busy schedule?

What specific challenges or needs do you currently face that require God's guidance and intervention?

Reflect on past experiences where prayer made a difference in your life. How did God answer your prayers, and what lessons can you learn from those experiences?

Prayer:

Dear God,

We thank You for the gift of prayer, which allows us to draw near to You in times of need. Teach us to approach You with open hearts, trusting in Your wisdom and provision. Help us prioritize prayer in our college journey, seeking Your guidance and finding comfort in Your presence. May our prayers be a source of strength and hope, knowing that You hear us and will provide the peace that surpasses all understanding.

Amen.

CAMPUS INVOLVEMENT

33

STEPPING OUT OF YOUR COMFORT ZONE

____ / ____ / _____

"Have I not commanded you? Be strong and courageous. Do not be afraid; do not be discouraged, for the Lord your God will be with you wherever you go."

- JOSHUA 1:9

As you embark on this journey of higher education, it's essential to embrace new opportunities and step out of your comfort zone. College is a time of discovery, a season where you can explore your passions, talents, and purpose. But often, that requires taking risks and venturing into unfamiliar territory.

Stepping out of your comfort zone might feel intimidating or uncomfortable, but remember that God has commanded you to be strong and courageous. He promises to be with you wherever you go, guiding and empowering you to embrace new opportunities.

Consider this: What passions lie dormant within you? What talents are waiting to be discovered? Be open to trying new things, whether it's joining a club, participating in a service project, or pursuing an interest outside of your academic studies. Don't let fear hold you back, for God has equipped you with the strength to overcome challenges and embrace growth.

The lessons you learn and the experiences you gain from stepping out of your comfort zone will shape you into the person God intends you to be. It's through these moments of exploration and risk-taking that you can discover your purpose and find fulfillment in the unique path God has laid before you.

Are there any opportunities you have hesitated to pursue due to fear or discomfort? What steps can you take to overcome those fears and embrace those opportunities?

How do you envision stepping out of your comfort zone contributing to your personal growth and the discovery of your passions and purpose?

In what ways can you rely on God's strength and presence as you navigate new experiences and challenges during your college journey?

Prayer:

Dear God,

Grant us the courage to step out of our comfort zones and embrace new opportunities. Help us overcome our fears and doubts, knowing that You are with us wherever we go. Guide us in discovering our passions, talents, and purpose, and may we find fulfillment in the unique path You have prepared for us. Strengthen us, O Lord, as we journey through college.

Amen.

34

FINDING YOUR NICHE AND STRENGTHS

___ / ___ / _____

"We have different gifts, according to the grace given to each of us. If your gift is prophesying, then prophesy in accordance with your faith; if it is serving, then serve; if it is teaching, then teach; if it is to encourage, then give encouragement; if it is giving, then give generously; if it is to lead, do it diligently; if it is to show mercy, do it cheerfully."

- ROMANS 12:6-8

Your campus is a bustling hub of diverse extracurricular activities and organizations, each offering unique opportunities for personal and skill development. As you navigate this landscape, it's important to find your niche and explore areas of interest that align with your strengths and passions.

God has bestowed each of us with different gifts, talents, and abilities. Take time to reflect on what you excel in and what brings you joy. Are you gifted in leadership, serving, teaching, encouragement, or other areas? Use these gifts as a compass to guide your exploration of extracurricular activities and organizations.

Engage in conversations with fellow students, attend information sessions, and participate in introductory meetings to get a sense of the various opportunities available. Seek guidance from mentors or upperclassmen who can offer insights based on their experiences. Remember, finding your niche is a journey, and it may take time and experimentation to discover where you truly belong.

When exploring extracurricular activities and organizations, be intentional about seeking the right fit. Consider your values, interests, and goals. Look for groups that align with your passions and provide opportunities for personal growth and development.

Remember that your involvement in extracurricular activities should not be solely for the sake of building a resume. It should be a chance to engage in meaningful experiences, connect with like-minded individuals, and make a positive impact on campus and in the community.

As you explore different options, remain open-minded and willing to step outside of your comfort zone. Sometimes, the most rewarding experiences come from unexpected places. Be willing to try new things, challenge yourself, and embrace the growth that comes with stepping into unfamiliar territory.

What are some of your natural talents and strengths? How can you incorporate them into your involvement in extracurricular activities?

What values and interests are important to you? How can you find organizations or activities that align with those values and interests?

In what ways do you hope to grow and develop through your participation in extracurricular activities and organizations?

Prayer:

Dear God,

Guide us as we explore the vast array of extracurricular activities and organizations available to us. Help us discern our passions, strengths, and values so that we may find the right fit. Open our hearts to new experiences and opportunities for growth. May our involvement be purposeful, bringing joy, fulfillment, and meaningful connections. Grant us wisdom as we navigate this journey of discovering our niche and contributing to the campus community.

Amen.

35

BALANCING COMMITMENTS

____ / ____ / _____

"Teach us to number our days, that we may gain a heart of wisdom."

- PSALM 90:12 (NIV)

F inding a balance between academic commitments, campus involvement, and personal life is crucial for a successful college experience. Without effective time management and prioritization, it's easy to become overwhelmed and experience negative consequences.

Imagine this scenario: You have a demanding course load, multiple extracurricular activities, part-time work, and social commitments. Without a clear plan and effective time management, you find yourself constantly rushing from one task to another, feeling stressed and exhausted. Your grades begin to suffer, and you struggle to keep up with assignments and deadlines. You feel torn between your academic responsibilities and your desire to be actively involved on campus. As a result, you may miss out on valuable opportunities for personal and professional growth.

To avoid such challenges, it's important to prioritize and manage your time effectively. Start by identifying your most important tasks and commitments. Set clear goals for your academic performance, involvement in campus activities, and personal well-being. Then, create a schedule that allocates dedicated time for each area of your life.

Practice the art of saying "no" when necessary. While it's tempting to take on every opportunity that comes your way, learn to assess whether it aligns with your priorities and capacity. Remember that it's okay to decline certain commitments to maintain a healthy balance.

Remember to schedule downtime and self-care activities as well. Taking breaks, engaging in hobbies, and nurturing relationships are vital for your overall well-being and can actually enhance your productivity and focus when you return to your responsibilities.

How do you currently manage your time and prioritize your commitments? Are there areas that need improvement?

What are your most important academic and personal goals? How can you align your commitments and time management strategies to support those goals?

What strategies can you implement to avoid the negative consequences of poor time management and achieve a better balance between your academic, campus, and personal life?

Prayer:

Dear God,

Grant us the wisdom and discipline to effectively manage our time and balance our commitments. Help us prioritize our academic responsibilities, campus involvement, and personal well-being in a way that honors You and brings about fruitful outcomes. Teach us to say "no" when necessary and guide us in making wise decisions about how to invest our time. Grant us peace and clarity as we navigate the challenges of balancing our various commitments. In Your name, we pray.

Amen.

———◆◇◆———

36

OVERCOMING FEAR OF FAILURE

____ / ____ / _____

"Have I not commanded you? Be strong and courageous. Do not be afraid; do not be discouraged, for the Lord your God will be with you wherever you go."

- JOSHUA 1:9 (NIV)

As you navigate the exciting and challenging journey of college, it's natural to experience moments of fear and doubt, especially when it comes to pursuing new opportunities. The fear of failure can be paralyzing, preventing us from stepping out of our comfort zones and embracing the risks that lead to personal growth.

In my own college years, I vividly remember the moment when I hesitated to join a campus organization. Thoughts of rejection, criticism, and the fear of not fitting in flooded my mind. The fear of failure whispered in my ear, urging me to play it safe and stay within the confines of my comfort zone.

But God's Word in Joshua 1:9 reminded me that He has commanded us to be strong and courageous. It's a command that resonates with every college student, urging us to face our fears head-on. With God by our side, we are called to step out in faith, trusting that He will provide guidance, strength, and support wherever we go.

As I found the courage to embrace the risk and join that organization, I discovered a world of new friendships, opportunities for personal growth, and a deeper sense of purpose. Yes, there were moments of setbacks and failures along the way, but each experience became a stepping stone toward growth and resilience. Through it all, I learned that failure does not define us; it refines us and equips us for future success.

So, I encourage you to step out of your comfort zones, even when fear tries to hold you back. Embrace the risks that come with pursuing your passions and seizing opportunities for personal and spiritual growth. Remember that God is with you every step of the way, empowering you to face your fears and experience transformative growth.

What opportunities or passions have you been hesitant to pursue due to fear of failure? How can you take a step forward despite the fear?

Reflect on a time when you faced failure or setbacks. How did it shape you and contribute to your personal growth?

How can you encourage and support your fellow college men in overcoming their fear of failure and embracing risks?

Prayer:

Dear God,

Grant us the strength and courage to overcome our fear of failure. Help us trust in Your presence and command to be strong and courageous. Guide us as we step out of our comfort zones, embracing the risks that lead to personal growth and spiritual maturity. In Jesus' name, we pray.

Amen.

———◄◦►———

37

TAKING ADVANTAGE OF COLLEGE RESOURCES

____ / ____ / _____

"Trust in the Lord with all your heart and lean not on your own under-standing; in all your ways submit to him, and he will make your paths straight."

- PROVERBS 3:5-6 (NIV)

Your college campus is filled with an abundance of resources and support systems designed to help you thrive academically, personally, and spiritually. Yet, it's all too easy to overlook or underutilize these valuable assets, relying solely on our own understanding and strength.

During my college journey, I encountered a semester filled with academic struggles. Overwhelmed and uncertain of how to improve, I found myself sinking deeper into self-doubt and frustration. Instead of seeking help, I fell into the trap of relying solely on my own abilities, thinking I could handle it alone.

It was in this moment that Proverbs 3:5-6 spoke to my heart. I realized that trust in the Lord required me to surrender my pride and submit to His guidance. With this newfound perspective, I humbled myself and sought the support of academic resources available on campus.

Through tutoring services, study groups, and professor consultations, I discovered a wealth of knowledge and guidance that I had been missing out on. By leveraging these resources and submitting my struggles to God, my understanding expanded, my grades improved, and I gained valuable insights into effective study habits and time management.

The lesson I learned was invaluable. College offers us a unique opportunity to access a wide range of resources, such as academic support, career services, counseling, and spiritual guidance. Utilizing these resources not only enhances our college experience but also equips us with the tools necessary for success and personal growth.

So, I encourage you to take full advantage of the resources and support systems available to you. Trust in the Lord with all your heart and recognize that seeking help is not a sign of weakness but a wise decision. By submitting to God's guidance and utilizing the resources at your disposal, you can navigate the challenges of college life with greater ease and confidence.

Reflect on the areas of your college life where you could benefit from utilizing available resources or seeking support. How can you take the first step in accessing those resources?

Share an experience when seeking help or guidance from a support system on campus positively impacted your college journey.

How can you encourage and support your fellow college men in maximizing the resources and support systems available to them?

Prayer:

Dear God,

We acknowledge that You have provided us with abundant resources and support systems on our college campuses. Help us trust in You and lean not on our own understanding. Grant us the wisdom to recognize our need for help and the courage to seek guidance and support. Guide us as we utilize these resources to enhance our academic, personal, and spiritual growth.

Amen.

38

EXPLORING INTERESTS AND PASSIONS

_____ / _____ / _____

"Delight yourself in the Lord, and he will give you the desires of your heart."

\- PSALM 37:4 (ESV)

In the midst of the busyness and demands of college life, it's crucial to remember the importance of exploring your personal interests and passions. While academics play a significant role in your journey, engaging in activities that bring you joy and fulfillment outside of your studies is equally valuable.

As a fellow college graduate who has walked a similar path, I want to share with you the transformative power of pursuing your interests and passions. There was a time when I became so focused on my academic goals that I neglected to make time for the things that truly ignited my soul. It took a toll on my well-being and left me feeling unfulfilled.

It was through the wisdom of Psalm 37:4 that I realized the significance of finding delight in the Lord and allowing Him to shape the desires of my heart. God created each of us uniquely, with diverse interests and talents. When we embrace and cultivate these passions, it not only brings us joy but also deepens our understanding of ourselves and God's purpose for our lives.

I encourage you to step outside the confines of your academic pursuits and explore the depths of your interests and passions. Take time to reflect on what truly brings you joy and fulfillment. It could be anything from playing a musical instrument, engaging in sports, pursuing creative arts, or volunteering for a cause close to your heart.

When we prioritize our passions alongside our academic commitments, we unlock a greater sense of balance, well-being, and personal growth. Embracing our interests not only enriches our college experience but also allows us to develop a more well-rounded and purposeful life.

So, my challenge to you is this: carve out time in your schedule to pursue your passions. Seek out opportunities to engage in activities that resonate with your soul. Embrace the unique talents and desires God has given you, knowing that as you delight in Him, He will guide you and fulfill the desires of your heart.

What are some interests or passions that you have neglected in the pursuit of academics? How can you begin to prioritize and make time for them?

Reflect on and share a specific moment when engaging in a personal interest or passion brought you a sense of joy and fulfillment.

How can you encourage and support your fellow college men in exploring their interests and passions?

Prayer:

Dear Heavenly Father,

Thank You for the passions and interests You have placed within each of us. Help us find delight in You and discover the desires of our hearts. Guide us as we explore and develop our personal interests, knowing that through these pursuits, we can grow closer to You and experience a more fulfilling college journey.

Amen.

PHYSICAL HEALTH

39

Nurturing Physical and Mental Well-being in College

___ / ___ / _____

"Beloved, I pray that all may go well with you and that you may be in good health, as it goes well with your soul."

- 3 John 1:2

College life can be a whirlwind of activities, responsibilities, and challenges. It's easy to get caught up in the demands of academics, social engagements, and personal responsibilities, often neglecting our physical and mental well-being in the process. However, it is essential to find balance and prioritize self-care in order to thrive holistically.

As a college student, you may encounter times when stress becomes overwhelming and your physical and mental health are at risk. It is during these moments that you must pause, reflect, and intentionally nurture your well-being. Remember that taking care of yourself is not selfish; it is an act of self-love and self-preservation.

Find time to engage in activities that bring you joy and peace, whether it's spending time in nature, practicing mindfulness, pursuing hobbies, or connecting with loved ones. Prioritize rest and sleep, as they are crucial for recharging your body and mind. Seek support from trusted friends, mentors, or campus resources when needed. By nurturing your physical and mental well-being, you can navigate college life with resilience and embrace the fullness of the experience.

What are some practical ways you can prioritize self-care and well-being in the midst of your college schedule?

How can you create a healthy balance between your academic responsibilities and personal well-being?

What support systems or resources are available to you on campus that can assist in nurturing your physical and mental health?

Prayer:

Dear God,

Grant me the wisdom to prioritize my physical and mental well-being amidst the demands of college life. Help me find balance, seek support when needed, and make choices that promote my overall health. May my journey through college be marked by a vibrant spirit, sound mind, and a healthy body.

Amen.

40

FUELING YOUR BODY FOR SUCCESS

____ / ____ / _____

"So, whether you eat or drink, or whatever you do, do all to the glory of God. "

- 1 CORINTHIANS 10:31

I t's easy to fall into unhealthy eating habits. Late-night study sessions, fast food runs, and irregular meal patterns can take a toll on your physical well-being and energy levels. However, nourishing your body with wholesome food is essential for optimal health and success.

As a college student, adopting healthy eating habits can positively impact your overall well-being and academic performance. Consider the importance of balanced nutrition, incorporating a variety of fruits, vegetables, whole grains, lean proteins, and healthy fats into your meals. Be mindful of portion sizes and practice moderation.

Meal planning and preparation can be helpful strategies to maintain healthy eating habits. Set aside time each week to plan your meals, create a grocery list, and prepare nutritious snacks. This can help you make conscious choices, save time, and avoid relying on unhealthy food options.

Remember that healthy eating is not about strict diets or depriving yourself of enjoyment. It's about fueling your body with nourishing food that provides energy and supports your well-being. By making mindful food choices, you can cultivate healthy eating habits that will sustain you throughout your college journey.

How can you incorporate more fruits, vegetables, and whole foods into your meals and snacks?

What are some strategies you can implement to plan and prepare healthy meals in your busy college schedule?

How does fueling your body with nutritious food impact your energy levels, focus, and overall well-being?

Prayer:

Dear Lord,

Guide me in making wise choices when it comes to my eating habits. Help me prioritize nutrition and make mindful food choices that nourish my body and fuel my mind. Give me the discipline to plan and prepare healthy meals, and may my eating habits reflect my desire to honor and glorify You in all that I do.

Amen.

41

FITNESS IN COLLEGE

_____ / _____ / _____

"Do you not know that your bodies are temples of the Holy Spirit, who is in you, whom you have received from God? You are not your own; you were bought at a price. Therefore, honor God with your bodies."

- 1 CORINTHIANS 6:19-20

College life is filled with countless demands on your time and energy, making it easy to neglect physical fitness. However, as someone who has journeyed through college and learned valuable lessons along the way, I want to encourage you to prioritize exercise and make it an integral part of your college experience.

Regular physical activity not only improves your physical health but also enhances your mental well-being, boosts your energy levels, and reduces stress. It can be a powerful tool in managing the challenges and demands of college life. Establishing exercise habits now will not only benefit you during your college years but also lay a foundation for a healthy lifestyle beyond graduation.

Start by identifying activities that you enjoy and that align with your schedule. It could be anything from jogging, cycling, dancing, or participating in sports. Find a gym or fitness center on campus, join intramural teams, or form workout groups with friends. Making exercise a social activity can bring motivation, accountability, and camaraderie.

It's important to remember that incorporating exercise into your routine doesn't have to be complicated or time-consuming. Even short bursts of physical activity can have significant benefits. Consider taking breaks during study sessions to stretch or do a quick workout. Walk or bike to class instead of relying solely on transportation. Take advantage of opportunities for movement throughout your day.

By prioritizing fitness, you're not only investing in your physical health but also honoring God with your bodies. Recognize that your body is a gift from God and a temple of the Holy Spirit. Taking care of it allows you to serve Him better, fulfill your purpose, and experience the fullness of life He has planned for you.

How can you incorporate physical activity into your daily routine, considering your interests and schedule?

What are some barriers or challenges you may face in prioritizing exercise, and how can you overcome them?

How does physical fitness impact your overall well-being, academic performance, and spiritual journey?

Prayer:

Dear Lord,

Help me prioritize my physical fitness and establish healthy exercise habits in my college years. Guide me in finding activities that bring me joy and align with my schedule. Strengthen my commitment to caring for my body, which is a temple of Your Holy Spirit. May my dedication to fitness reflect my desire to honor You in all aspects of my life.

Amen.

—◦—

42

PRIORITIZING SLEEP

___ / ___ / _____

"In peace I will lie down and sleep, for you alone, Lord, make me dwell in safety."

- PSALM 4:8

As someone who has navigated the challenges of college life, I understand how easy it is to sacrifice sleep in the pursuit of academic success and social activities. However, I want to emphasize the importance of prioritizing rest and developing healthy sleep habits for your physical and mental well-being.

Quality sleep plays a vital role in your overall health and performance. It affects your cognitive function, memory retention, mood regulation, and immune system. Without adequate sleep, you may experience difficulties concentrating, increased stress levels, compromised immune function, and a decline in academic performance.

To prioritize sleep hygiene, establish a consistent sleep schedule by going to bed and waking up at the same time each day, even on weekends. Create a sleep-friendly environment by ensuring your bedroom is cool, dark, and quiet. Minimize exposure to electronic devices before bedtime, as the blue light emitted from screens can interfere with your sleep quality.

Engaging in relaxation techniques such as deep breathing, meditation, or reading a book before bed can help calm your mind and prepare your body for rest. Avoid consuming caffeine or heavy meals close to bedtime, as they can disrupt your sleep patterns. Instead, opt for a soothing herbal tea or light snack if needed.

Remember, sleep is not a luxury but a necessity for your overall well-being. By prioritizing rest, you're investing in your physical health, mental clarity, and academic success. Trust in the Lord's provision and find comfort in knowing that He offers a place of safety and peace in the embrace of sleep.

How can you establish a consistent sleep schedule that aligns with your college routine?

What activities or habits can you incorporate into your evening routine to promote relaxation and prepare your mind and body for restful sleep?

Reflect on the times when lack of sleep affected your academic performance or overall well-being. How can you make changes to prioritize sleep moving forward?

Prayer:

Dear Lord,

I thank You for the gift of sleep and the rest it provides for my body and mind. Help me prioritize my sleep and develop healthy sleep habits in college. Guide me in creating a peaceful environment and establishing a consistent sleep routine. Grant me the wisdom to make choices that promote rest and optimal performance. In Your loving care, I find safety and peace.

Amen.

43

Screen Time

____ / ____ / _____

"I will set no worthless thing before my eyes; I hate the work of those who fall away; it shall not fasten its grip on me."

- Psalm 101:3 (NASB)

Today's digital age has a strong grip over us, constantly tempting us to spend time looking at screens for a myriad of reasons. However, it is important to find a balance and take care of both your eyes and mind by managing your screen time effectively.

Excessive screen time can have negative impacts on your physical and mental health. Prolonged exposure to screens can strain your eyes, leading to eye fatigue, dryness, and even vision problems. Additionally, spending excessive time on electronic devices can contribute to feelings of anxiety, depression, and decreased productivity.

To maintain a healthy balance, consider implementing strategies to limit your screen time. Set boundaries by scheduling designated screen-free periods throughout your day. Use that time to engage in activities that promote your well-being, such as spending time in nature, pursuing hobbies, or connecting with friends face-to-face.

Practice mindful technology use by being intentional about the content you consume and the platforms you engage with. Avoid mindlessly scrolling through social media or getting caught up in comparison and negative online environments. Instead, seek out educational resources, inspiring content, and opportunities for personal growth.

Make a conscious effort to prioritize screen-free activities that bring you joy and fulfillment. This could include reading books, pursuing artistic or creative endeavors, engaging in physical exercise, or volunteering in your community. By finding a healthy balance, you can nurture your eyes and mind, leading to improved overall well-being.

Reflect on your current screen time habits. Are there any areas where you could make adjustments to create a healthier balance?

What screen-free activities bring you joy and fulfillment? How can you incorporate more of these activities into your daily routine?

Consider the impact excessive screen time has had on your mental and physical health. How can you make intentional choices to prioritize your well-being moving forward?

Prayer:

Dear Lord,

I seek Your guidance in finding a healthy balance in my screen time. Help me manage my technology use wisely and set boundaries that prioritize my physical and mental well-being. Grant me discernment to choose uplifting content and to engage in activities that nurture my soul. Protect my eyes from strain and my mind from the negative effects of excessive screen exposure. In Your presence, I find clarity and peace.

Amen.

44

Substance Use and Abuse

"Do not get drunk on wine, which leads to debauchery. Instead, be filled with the Spirit."

- Ephesians 5:18

College can be a time of experimentation and peer influence, but it's important to remember the potential risks and consequences associated with substance use. Alcohol and drugs may offer temporary relief or a sense of escape, but they can also lead to addiction, poor decision-making, impaired judgment, damaged relationships, and hindered academic performance.

Making informed choices means educating yourself about the risks and effects of substances, understanding your personal boundaries, and being intentional about your well-being. Surround yourself with friends who respect your choices and share similar values. Seek support from campus resources, such as counseling services or student organizations that promote healthy lifestyles.

Embrace a holistic approach to your well-being by focusing on self-care, engaging in meaningful activities, and cultivating a supportive community. Explore alternative ways to have fun and relieve stress without relying on substances, such as participating in sports, joining clubs, or pursuing creative outlets.

Remember, your body is a temple, and it is your responsibility to honor and care for it. By making informed choices and rejecting harmful substances, you can experience the fullness of life and be filled with the Spirit's guidance, wisdom, and joy.

Reflect on your personal boundaries and values regarding substance use. How can you communicate and uphold these boundaries in social settings?

Consider the potential risks and consequences associated with substance abuse. How can you prioritize your health and well-being by making informed choices?

Reflect on healthy alternatives to substance use for stress relief and enjoyment. What activities or hobbies bring you fulfillment and promote your overall well-being?

Prayer:

Dear Lord,

I seek Your wisdom and strength in making informed choices about substance use. Help me understand the risks and consequences involved and grant me the courage to stand firm in my values. Surround me with friends who support my well-being and provide opportunities for me to engage in fulfilling activities. Fill me with Your Spirit, guiding me toward a life of purpose and joy.

Amen.

MENTAL WELL-BEING

45

EMBRACING REST AND SABBATH

_____ / _____ / _____

"Remember the Sabbath day by keeping it holy."

- EXODUS 20:8

You're a college student navigating through the hectic demands of assignments, exams, and social commitments. This means your days are filled with constant busyness, leaving little time for rest and reflection. But in the midst of this chaos, have you considered the importance of embracing the Sabbath?

The concept of Sabbath is deeply rooted in biblical principles. It is a time set apart for rest, reflection, and spiritual renewal. Just as God rested on the seventh day after creating the world, He invites us to experience the benefits of Sabbath in our lives.

Embracing Sabbath doesn't necessarily mean following strict rules or rituals. It's about intentionally creating space for rest and spiritual nourishment. It's a time to disconnect from the demands of college life and reconnect with your faith, your purpose, and yourself.

Use this time to engage in activities that bring you joy and rejuvenate your soul. Spend time in nature, immerse yourself in prayer and meditation, read uplifting books, or engage in worship. Embrace solitude and allow your mind to find stillness amidst the noise of college life.

By embracing Sabbath, you'll discover a renewed sense of purpose, clarity, and peace. It's a reminder that you are not defined solely by your academic achievements or social status. Your worth comes from being a beloved child of God, and He desires for you to experience true rest and spiritual growth.

How do you currently prioritize rest and spiritual renewal in your college routine? Are there any adjustments you can make to embrace Sabbath more intentionally?

Reflect on the benefits of rest and reflection in your life. How does Sabbath practice contribute to your overall well-being and personal growth?

Consider practical steps you can take to incorporate Sabbath practices into your college life. What activities or rituals can you establish to find spiritual renewal and refreshment?

Prayer:

Dear God,

Thank You for the gift of Sabbath. Help me to embrace this practice in my college life, finding rest and spiritual renewal in Your presence. Guide me in creating space for reflection and disconnecting from the busyness around me. May Sabbath become a source of peace, joy, and spiritual growth.

Amen.

46

PRACTICING SELF-CARE

___ / ___ / _____

"For we are God's handiwork, created in Christ Jesus to do good works, which God prepared in advance for us to do."

- EPHESIANS 2:10

With academic pressures, social expectations, and personal challenges taking a toll on your well-being, college life can be overwhelming. In the midst of it all, it's crucial to practice self-care and nurture your inner self and self-worth.

Practicing self-care goes beyond simply indulging in temporary pleasures. It's about recognizing your inherent worth as a child of God and prioritizing your physical, emotional, and spiritual needs. It's a deliberate act of self-compassion and acceptance.

Nurturing your inner self starts with cultivating a healthy mindset. Replace self-criticism with self-encouragement and self-acceptance. Remember that you are fearfully and wonderfully made, with unique gifts and talents to contribute to the world.

Take time to engage in activities that bring you joy and fulfillment. Pursue hobbies, spend time with loved ones, and explore your passions outside of academic demands. Establish healthy boundaries and learn to say no to activities or commitments that drain your energy and detract from your well-being.

Seek support when needed. Reach out to trusted friends, mentors, or campus resources for guidance and encouragement. Remember, it's not a sign of weakness to ask for help. Surround yourself with a supportive community that uplifts and celebrates your journey.

By practicing self-care, you are better equipped to navigate the challenges of college life and fulfill the purpose God has for you. Nurturing your inner self and self-worth allows you to approach your studies, relationships, and personal growth with a healthier perspective and greater resilience.

How do you currently practice self-care in your college life? Are there any areas where you can prioritize your well-being more intentionally?

Reflect on the impact of self-compassion and self-acceptance in your life. How does nurturing your inner self contribute to your overall well-being and personal growth?

Consider practical steps you can take to enhance self-care in your daily routine. How can you prioritize your physical, emotional, and spiritual needs?

Prayer:

Dear God,

Thank You for creating me as Your handiwork. Help me to practice self-care and nurture my inner self and self-worth. Teach me to be kind and compassionate toward myself, embracing my strengths and accepting my limitations. Guide me in making healthy choices and surrounding myself with a supportive community. May I find fulfillment and joy in nurturing my well-being.

Amen.

47

DEVELOPING EMOTIONAL RESILIENCE

____ / ____ / _____

"Consider it pure joy, my brothers and sisters, whenever you face trials of many kinds, because you know that the testing of your faith produces perseverance."

- JAMES 1:2-3

College life is full of challenges, both academically and personally. It's easy to feel overwhelmed and discouraged when facing setbacks and adversity. However, developing emotional resilience is key to building strength and coping skills.

Emotional resilience is the ability to bounce back from difficulties, to adapt and grow through life's challenges. It's not about avoiding pain or pretending that everything is fine, but rather about developing healthy ways to navigate and overcome hardships.

In college, you'll encounter academic pressures, relationship struggles, and unexpected hurdles. Instead of allowing these challenges to define you, view them as opportunities for growth. Embrace the mindset that trials can produce perseverance and ultimately strengthen your faith.

Building emotional resilience starts with acknowledging and understanding your emotions. Allow yourself to feel and process them without judgment or suppression. Seek healthy outlets for expression, such as journaling, talking with trusted friends, or seeking professional support if needed.

Cultivate a support system of friends, mentors, and community who can provide encouragement and wisdom during difficult times. Surround yourself with positive influences that uplift and inspire you to overcome obstacles.

Develop healthy coping mechanisms to manage stress and build resilience. This may include practicing mindfulness, engaging in physical exercise, pursuing hobbies, or finding solace in prayer and meditation. Each person's journey is unique, so explore what works best for you.

Remember, emotional resilience is a lifelong journey. It takes time and practice to develop these skills. Trust in God's faithfulness and seek His guidance as you navigate through challenges. He is with you every step of the way, providing strength and comfort.

How do you currently handle adversity and setbacks in your college life? Are there any areas where you can develop greater emotional resilience?

Reflect on the role of faith in building emotional resilience. How does your relationship with God contribute to your ability to persevere through trials?

Consider practical steps you can take to enhance your coping skills and emotional resilience. What healthy outlets and support systems can you establish?

Prayer:

Dear God,

Thank You for the promise of emotional resilience. Help me to develop strength and coping skills to navigate the challenges of college life. Grant me wisdom to understand my emotions and the courage to face adversity with faith. Surround me with a supportive community that encourages growth and provides comfort. May I find strength and perseverance through You.

Amen.

48

THE POWER OF YOUR THOUGHTS

___ / ___ / _____

"Finally, brothers and sisters, whatever is true, whatever is noble, whatever is right, whatever is pure, whatever is lovely, whatever is admirable—if anything is excellent or praiseworthy—think about such things."

- PHILIPPIANS 4:8

Your thoughts and emotions have a powerful impact on your mental and emotional state. They influence your perception of yourself, your circumstances, and the world around you. By renewing your thoughts and emotions, you can experience a transformative shift in your mindset.

Start by becoming aware of your thoughts. Notice when negative or self-defeating thoughts arise and consciously choose to replace them with positive and affirming ones. Focus on thoughts that are true, noble, right, pure, lovely, admirable, excellent, and praiseworthy, as the verse from Philippians encourages.

Renewing your mind with God's truth and promises is essential for cultivating a positive mindset. Fill your mind with Scripture, meditate on God's Word, and seek His guidance in prayer. Allow His truth to shape your thoughts and emotions, replacing negativity with hope, gratitude, and faith.

Practice self-compassion and extend grace to yourself. College life can be overwhelming, and it's normal to experience moments of doubt, stress, or insecurity. Remember that you are fearfully and wonderfully made by God, and your worth is not determined by external achievements or circumstances.

Surround yourself with positive influences and supportive relationships. Engage in activities that uplift and inspire you, such as pursuing hobbies, spending time in nature, or serving others. Cultivate a gratitude practice, intentionally focusing on the blessings and goodness in your life.

As you cultivate a positive mindset, you'll find that your overall well-being improves. You'll become more resilient in the face of challenges, more open to new opportunities, and better equipped to navigate the ups and downs of college life.

Reflect on your current thought patterns and emotional tendencies. Are there any negative or self-defeating thoughts that you can replace with positive and affirming ones?

How does your faith in God's promises impact your mindset? How can you incorporate more of His truth into your thoughts and emotions?

Consider practical ways you can cultivate a positive mindset in your daily life. What activities, practices, or relationships can contribute to your overall positivity?

Prayer:

Dear God,

Thank You for the power of renewing my thoughts and emotions. Help me to cultivate a positive mindset that aligns with Your truth and promises. Guide me in replacing negative thoughts with positive and affirming ones. Fill me with gratitude, hope, and faith. Surround me with positive influences and supportive relationships. May my mindset reflect Your goodness and transform my college experience.

Amen.

49

NAVIGATING STRESS AND ANXIETY

___ / ___ / _____

"Do not be anxious about anything, but in every situation, by prayer and petition, with thanksgiving, present your requests to God. And the peace of God, which transcends all understanding, will guard your hearts and your minds in Christ Jesus."

- PHILIPPIANS 4:6-7

When stress and anxiety arise, it's important to recognize that you are not alone. Many college students face similar challenges and emotions. Remember that it is okay to seek help and support. Take the time to identify healthy coping mechanisms that work for you, whether it's practicing deep breathing exercises, engaging in physical activity, journaling, or spending time in prayer and meditation.

In the midst of college pressures, it can be easy to neglect self-care. However, prioritizing self-care is vital for maintaining emotional well-being. Make time for activities that recharge and refresh you, such as hobbies, spending time in nature, or engaging in meaningful relationships. Remember to rest and find a healthy balance between your academic responsibilities and personal life.

Additionally, seek support from your community. Surround yourself with friends, mentors, and spiritual leaders who can provide encouragement and guidance. Share your struggles and concerns with trusted individuals who can offer a listening ear and help you navigate through challenging times. Don't hesitate to reach out for professional help when needed, as counseling services and mental health resources are often available on campus.

Ultimately, as a college student, your faith can be a source of strength and comfort. Turn to God in prayer, casting your anxieties and worries upon Him. Seek His guidance and wisdom in navigating through college pressures. Trust that He will provide peace that surpasses all understanding, guarding your heart and mind.

How do you currently manage stress and anxiety in your college life? Are there any areas where you can incorporate healthier coping mechanisms?

Reflect on the role of faith in finding peace amidst college pressures. How can you rely on God's promises and seek His guidance in managing stress and anxiety?

Consider practical steps you can take to prioritize self-care and seek support from your community. Who can you reach out to for encouragement and guidance?

Prayer:

Dear God,

I come before You with my stress and anxiety. Grant me peace in the midst of college pressures. Help me to navigate challenges with wisdom and resilience. Guide me to healthy coping mechanisms and self-care practices. Surround me with a supportive community that uplifts and encourages me. May Your peace guard my heart and mind.

Amen.

50

SEEKING PROFESSIONAL HELP

____ / ____ / _____

"Plans fail for lack of counsel, but with many advisers, they succeed."

- PROVERBS 15:22

College can be an exciting and transformative time, but it can also bring its share of challenges and struggles. When facing difficulties related to mental health and well-being, it's crucial to seek professional help and utilize the resources available on campus.

Many colleges offer counseling services, health centers, and support groups specifically designed to support students' mental health needs. These resources provide a safe and confidential space to address concerns, process emotions, and receive guidance from trained professionals.

As college men, it's important to adopt a proactive approach to mental health. Recognize that seeking professional help is not a sign of weakness but a courageous step toward self-care and growth. By reaching out to counselors or therapists, you can gain valuable insights, develop coping strategies, and receive the support you need to navigate through challenging times.

In addition to professional help, your college community can also serve as a source of support. Engage with campus organizations, clubs, or faith-based groups that align with your interests and values. Surrounding yourself with a network of peers who share similar experiences can provide a sense of belonging and understanding.

Remember that seeking professional help is a journey, and it may take time to find the right resources and professionals who resonate with you. Be patient with yourself and trust that there is support available to guide you through difficult seasons.

How comfortable are you with seeking professional help for your mental health? Are there any stigmas or misconceptions that hinder you from reaching out?

Reflect on the potential benefits of counseling or therapy. What areas of your mental health and well-being could benefit from professional guidance?

Consider the campus resources available to you. How can you actively seek and utilize these resources to support your mental health and well-being?

Prayer:

Dear God,

I acknowledge the importance of seeking professional help for my mental health and well-being. Grant me the courage to reach out and utilize the resources available on campus. Guide me to professionals who can provide valuable insights and support. Help me to be proactive in my approach to mental health, seeking the guidance I need for growth and healing.

Amen.

PERSONAL DEVELOPMENT

51

EMBRACING SELF-DISCOVERY

_____ / _____ / _____

"For we are God's handiwork, created in Christ Jesus to do good works, which God prepared in advance for us to do."

- EPHESIANS 2:10

As you embark on this journey of personal growth during your college years, I want to share with you the importance of embracing self-discovery. This is a time of immense opportunity, a time to explore your passions, talents, and values. It is a time to discover who you are and who God has created you to be.

In college, you have the unique privilege of taking ownership of your education. It is not just about acquiring knowledge and earning a degree; it is about discovering your purpose and fulfilling the calling that God has placed upon your life. Each day presents an opportunity to learn, to grow, and to develop your character.

As you navigate this journey of self-discovery, remember that it is not solely about achieving external success or conforming to societal expectations. It is about aligning your pursuits with your God-given gifts and values. Take time to reflect on what truly brings you joy and fulfillment, and pursue those passions wholeheartedly.

Embrace the process of self-discovery with an open mind and a willing spirit. Step out of your comfort zone and explore new experiences, join clubs or organizations that align with your interests, and engage in meaningful conversations with others who have different perspectives. Embracing diversity and expanding your horizons will broaden your understanding of the world and enrich your personal growth.

Do not be discouraged by setbacks or uncertainties along the way. Remember that personal growth is a lifelong journey, and each experience, whether positive or challenging, contributes to your development. Trust in God's plan for your life, knowing that He has created you with a unique purpose and has prepared good works in advance for you to do.

How are you currently embracing self-discovery in your college journey? Are there any areas where you feel hesitant or unsure about exploring your passions and values?

Reflect on the verse from Ephesians 2:10. How does knowing that you are God's handiwork and that He has prepared good works for you to do impact your perspective on personal growth?

Consider practical steps you can take to actively engage in self-discovery. How can you create space for reflection, explore new opportunities, and surround yourself with a supportive community?

Prayer:

Dear God,

I thank You for the gift of personal growth and self-discovery. Help me to embrace this journey during my college years. Guide me in exploring my passions, talents, and values. Grant me wisdom and discernment as I seek to align my pursuits with Your plan for my life. Open my heart and mind to new experiences and opportunities for growth.

Amen.

52

CULTIVATING INTEGRITY AND MORAL VALUES

____ / ____ / _____

"But let your 'Yes' be 'Yes,' and your 'No,' 'No.' For whatever is more than these is from the evil one."

- MATTHEW 5:37

As you navigate the transformative years of college, it is essential to focus on building character and cultivating integrity. The choices you make and the values you uphold will shape the person you become and the impact you have on those around you.

I knew a young man named Caleb who entered college with a strong moral compass and a desire to live a life of integrity. He was faced with various temptations, peer pressure, and opportunities that could compromise his values. However, Caleb remained steadfast in his commitment to live a life aligned with his beliefs.

In one particular instance, Caleb was invited to participate in a dishonest act that could have yielded personal gain but at the expense of someone else. Despite the allure of the situation, Caleb chose to uphold his integrity and make a wise choice based on his moral values.

This experience taught Caleb a valuable lesson about the importance of character. He realized that building character is not just about doing what is right when it is convenient or easy; it is about making consistent choices that align with your principles, even in the face of temptation.

The verse from Matthew 5:37 reminds us of the power of our words and the importance of being people of integrity. It encourages us to let our yes be yes and our no be no, speaking and acting with honesty and authenticity.

As men, it is crucial to reflect on the values and principles that guide your life. Take time to identify your core beliefs and commit to living them out with consistency and integrity. Surround yourself with friends who share similar values and hold each other accountable.

Reflect on a time when you faced a moral dilemma or temptation in college. How did you respond? What were the factors that influenced your decision?

Consider the verse from Matthew 5:37. How does it speak to you about the importance of integrity and keeping your word? How can you apply this principle in your college journey?

Evaluate your current choices and actions. Are they aligned with your values and beliefs? Are there any areas where you need to make adjustments to cultivate greater integrity?

Prayer:

Dear God,

I thank You for the gift of moral values and integrity. Help me to build my character and cultivate a life of integrity in all that I do. Give me the strength to make wise choices that align with my beliefs, even when faced with challenges or temptations. Surround me with friends who encourage and support me in living a life of integrity.

Amen.

53

ADAPTABILITY

____ / ____ / _____

"For I know the plans I have for you," declares the Lord, "plans to prosper you and not to harm you, plans to give you hope and a future."

- JEREMIAH 29:11

During college, you will encounter numerous transitions and changes. From moving to a new campus, adjusting to a different routine, and forming new relationships, adaptability becomes a crucial skill to navigate these transitions with confidence.

There was a young man named Ryan who entered college with a sense of excitement but also apprehension about the unknown. As he began his freshman year, he faced challenges in adapting to the new environment, making friends, and managing the academic workload.

At first, Ryan felt overwhelmed and uncertain, unsure of how to navigate the changes. However, as time passed, he realized that adaptability was not about completely changing who he was, but rather about embracing the opportunities for growth and trusting in God's plans for his life.

The verse from Jeremiah 29:11 reminded Ryan of God's faithfulness and His plans for his future. It reassured him that even in the midst of uncertainty, God had a purpose and a hope-filled future for him.

Through this experience, Ryan learned the lesson of embracing change with confidence. He discovered that transitions provide opportunities for personal and spiritual growth, allowing him to develop resilience and adaptability in the process.

As college men, you too will encounter various transitions throughout your college journey. Embrace change as an opportunity for growth, relying on your faith and trust in God's plans. Seek support from friends, mentors, and campus resources to navigate the challenges that come with transitions.

Reflect on a transition or change you have experienced since starting college. How did you initially respond to it? How did you adapt and grow through that transition?

Meditate on Jeremiah 29:11. How does this verse give you confidence and hope in times of change and uncertainty? How can you apply this truth to your current situation?

Consider areas in your life where you may need to cultivate greater adaptability. What steps can you take to embrace change and navigate transitions with confidence?

Prayer:

Dear God,

I thank You for Your plans and purposes for my life. Help me to embrace change and navigate transitions with confidence, knowing that You are with me every step of the way. Grant me the wisdom and resilience to adapt to new environments and situations. Strengthen my faith and trust in You as I journey through college and beyond.

Amen.

54

DEVELOPING EMOTIONAL
INTELLIGENCE

____ / ____ / _____

"Above all else, guard your heart, for everything you do flows from it."

- PROVERBS 4:23

Developing emotional intelligence is a vital aspect of personal growth. Emotional intelligence involves self-awareness, empathy, and effective communication, which are key in building healthy relationships and navigating social dynamics.

When Jason entered college he was filled with excitement but found himself struggling to connect with others. He realized that his lack of emotional intelligence hindered his ability to understand and empathize with those around him. As he reflected on his experiences, he recognized the importance of cultivating self-awareness and empathy.

Jason began to take ownership of his emotional growth, seeking to understand his own emotions and how they impacted his interactions with others. He realized that self-awareness allowed him to respond more thoughtfully and empathetically, fostering deeper connections and resolving conflicts in a healthier way.

The verse from Proverbs 4:23 reminded Jason of the significance of guarding his heart. It prompted him to be mindful of his emotions, thoughts, and intentions, recognizing that they influence his actions and relationships. Through cultivating emotional intelligence, Jason learned to navigate social dynamics with greater understanding and compassion.

I encourage you to take ownership of your emotional growth. Cultivate self-awareness by regularly reflecting on your emotions, triggers, and responses. Seek to understand the experiences and perspectives of others, practicing empathy and active listening. Develop effective communication skills to express your thoughts and emotions authentically, while also considering the impact on others.

Reflect on a situation where you struggled to connect with someone or experienced conflict. How could emotional intelligence have influenced the outcome? What steps can you take to enhance your self-awareness and empathy in similar situations?

Meditate on Proverbs 4:23. How does guarding your heart contribute to the development of emotional intelligence? In what ways can this verse guide your interactions with others?

Consider a relationship that could benefit from improved emotional intelligence. How can you cultivate empathy and effective communication to strengthen that connection?

Prayer:

Dear God,

I seek Your guidance in developing emotional intelligence. Help me to grow in self-awareness, empathy, and effective communication. Grant me the wisdom to guard my heart, that my actions and relationships may reflect Your love and grace. May I be an instrument of peace and understanding in the midst of social dynamics.

Amen.

55

GROWING SELF-CONFIDENCE

____ / ____ / _____

"For you created my inmost being; you knit me together in my mother's womb. I praise you because I am fearfully and wonderfully made; your works are wonderful, I know that full well."

\- Psalm 139:13-14

N ever underestimate the power of growing self-confidence and embracing your identity and potential. Recognize that you are fearfully and wonderfully made, uniquely designed by God for a purpose.

I knew a young man named Michael who entered college feeling uncertain about his abilities and comparing himself to others. He struggled with self-doubt, questioning whether he belonged or had what it took to succeed. However, through personal reflection and spiritual growth, he learned the importance of embracing his identity in Christ.

Michael realized that his worth and potential were not determined by external achievements or societal standards. He understood that his true value came from being a child of God, created with unique gifts and talents. This realization ignited a sense of self-confidence within him.

Instead of focusing on comparison, Michael began to embrace his strengths and abilities. He discovered that when he fully embraced his identity and potential, he was able to contribute to his college community in meaningful ways and pursue his passions with greater purpose.

I encourage you to embrace your identity and potential in Christ. Recognize that your worth is not defined by external accomplishments or the opinions of others. Instead, find confidence in knowing that God has created you for a purpose and has equipped you with unique gifts and talents.

Pursue your passions, explore your interests, and seek opportunities for personal and professional growth. Remember that your journey is unique, and you have the ability to make a significant impact on the world around you.

Reflect on a time when self-doubt hindered your ability to embrace your identity and potential. How did it impact your mindset and actions? What steps can you take to cultivate self-confidence and embrace who you are in Christ?

Meditate on Psalm 139:13-14. How does this verse affirm your worth and potential? How can you integrate this truth into your daily life and interactions with others?

Consider an area of your life where you would like to grow in confidence.

How can you leverage your unique gifts and talents in that area? What steps can you take to pursue personal and professional growth?

Prayer:

Dear God,

I thank You for creating me fearfully and wonderfully. Help me to embrace my identity and potential in Christ. Give me the confidence to pursue my passions, knowing that You have equipped me with unique gifts and talents. May I use them to make a positive impact on the world around me.

Amen.

56

———◄◆O◆►———

BUILDING LEADERSHIP SKILLS

____ / ____ / _____

*"But among you it will be different. Whoever wants to be a leader
among you must be your servant."*

\- MARK 10:43

It's crucial to recognize that leadership goes beyond titles or positions. True leadership is about serving others and using your influence to bring about positive change.

Leadership is not confined to specific roles or positions; it's a mindset and a set of skills that anyone can develop. It's about recognizing opportunities to serve others and making a meaningful impact wherever you find yourself.

The verse from Mark 10:43 reminds us of a fundamental truth: leadership requires humility and a servant's heart. To be a leader, you must be willing to put others before yourself, serving them with sincerity and compassion. This principle should guide your actions and decisions as you seek to lead with integrity and make a positive difference in the lives of those around you.

So, how can you cultivate your leadership skills and make a difference on your college campus? First, seek out opportunities for growth and learning. Engage in activities, organizations, or projects that align with your passions and values. Surround yourself with mentors and like-minded individuals who can guide and inspire you on your leadership journey.

Additionally, focus on developing essential skills such as effective communication, problem-solving, and collaboration. These skills will enable you to lead with confidence and navigate the challenges that arise during your college years. Remember, leadership is a continuous process of growth and self-improvement.

As you reflect on your college experience, think about the areas where you feel passionate about making a difference. It could be within a specific organization, a community project, or even among your peers. Use your influence and leadership skills to initiate positive change in those areas. Inspire others to join you in creating a better environment for everyone.

In conclusion, embrace your role as a leader. And remember, true leadership starts from within and is rooted in a sincere desire to serve and uplift others.

How do you define leadership? What are some qualities or characteristics you admire in effective leaders?

Reflect on Mark 10:43. How can you apply the principle of servant leadership to your own life and leadership journey?

Identify one area in your college experience where you can make a positive difference. How can you use your influence and leadership skills to bring about change in that area?

Prayer:

Dear God,

I seek Your guidance and wisdom as I develop my leadership skills. Help me to lead with humility, compassion, and a servant's heart. Show me the opportunities where I can make a positive difference during my college years. May my leadership be a reflection of Your love and grace.

Amen

RELATIONSHIPS AND DATING

57

BALANCING COLLEGE LIFE AND HOME CONNECTIONS

___ / ___ / _____

"Honor your father and your mother, so that you may live long in the land the LORD your God is giving you."

- EXODUS 20:12

While you're having fun at college, it's essential to remember the significance of maintaining relationships with your family and old friends. Balancing the demands of college life with your connections back home can be challenging, but it's worth the effort to nurture these important relationships.

The verse from Exodus 20:12 reminds us of the commandment to honor our parents. While in college, it's crucial to communicate regularly with your family and express gratitude for their support. Even though you may be physically apart, staying connected through phone calls, video chats, or visits during breaks can strengthen the bond and provide a sense of belonging.

Similarly, old friendships hold a special place in our lives. These are the friends who have known us for years and have shared precious memories with us. Despite the distance and the changes that college brings, intentional efforts must be made to maintain these connections. Reach out to them, plan reunions, and cherish the moments you spend together.

Navigating the balance between college life and maintaining relationships requires effective communication and time management. Schedule regular check-ins with your loved ones and make the most of the moments you have together. Being present in those conversations and genuinely showing interest in their lives will deepen the connection and create lasting memories.

It's also important to understand that relationships evolve, and adjustments are necessary. College is a transformative time, and both you and your loved ones will experience growth and change. Embrace these changes, celebrate each other's accomplishments, and support one another through the challenges that arise.

You'll thank yourself if you maintain relationships with your family and old friends. Honor your parents by staying connected and expressing gratitude for their love and support. Nurture your old friendships, investing time and effort to keep the bond alive. Through effective communication and intentional actions, you can strike a balance between college life and home connections, enriching your overall college experience. There will be a time you go home and wish you had.

How have your relationships with family and old friends impacted your college journey so far? What are some ways you can strengthen these connections?

Reflect on Exodus 20:12. What does it mean to honor your parents while in college? How can you show gratitude and maintain a strong relationship with them?

Identify one old friend or family member you haven't connected with in a while and take a stop toward connecting again. What intentional actions can you take to reconnect and nurture that relationship?

Prayer:

Dear God,

Thank You for the gift of family and old friends. Help me to honor my parents and stay connected with them despite the distance. Guide me in nurturing my relationships with old friends and cherishing the memories we share. Grant me wisdom and grace to balance college life with maintaining these important connections.

Amen.

58

THE SINGLE SEASON

_____ / _____ / _____

"Delight yourself in the LORD, and he will give you the desires of your heart."

- PSALM 37:4

I want to talk to you about the season of singleness and the incredible opportunity it presents. Embracing your singleness during your college years allows you to focus on personal growth, deepen your relationship with God, discover your purpose in Him, and discern the right romantic partner for your future.

While it is natural to desire companionship and seek romantic relationships, the single season offers a unique chance to find contentment and fulfillment in God alone. The verse from Psalm 37:4 reminds us that when we delight ourselves in the Lord, He aligns our desires with His will, and He provides what is best for us.

Instead of rushing into relationships out of loneliness or societal pressure, take this time to grow in self-awareness and seek God's guidance in choosing a partner. Use your single season to develop a strong foundation in your faith and understand your values and priorities. Seek a partner who shares your beliefs, complements your strengths, and supports your dreams.

During this season, focus on cultivating qualities that will contribute to a healthy and loving relationship. Work on your character, emotional intelligence, and communication skills. Seek wisdom from godly mentors and trusted friends who can provide guidance as you navigate the journey of relationships.

While waiting for the right person, be patient and trust in God's timing. Remember that your worth and identity are found in Christ, not in a romantic partner. Allow God to shape your heart and prepare you for a relationship that aligns with His plan and purpose for your life.

In conclusion, embrace your single season with joy and purpose. Delight yourself in the Lord, seeking His will above all else. Use this time to grow in faith, discover your purpose, make a positive impact, and discern the right romantic partner. Trust in God's plan for your life and seek His guidance in all relationships.

How can you balance the desire for a romantic partner with the need to embrace your single season and focus on personal growth?

Reflect on Psalm 37:4. How can delighting yourself in the Lord help you in discerning the right romantic partner?

Identify the qualities and values you seek in a future partner. How can you develop those qualities in yourself during your single season?

Prayer:

Dear God,

Thank You for this season of singleness. Help me to embrace it with joy and purpose. Guide me in delighting myself in You and seeking Your will above all else. Give me wisdom and discernment as I navigate the journey of relationships. Prepare my heart for a future partner who aligns with Your plan and purpose for my life.

Amen.

59

SEEKING GOD'S GUIDANCE IN RELATIONSHIPS

_____ / _____ / _____

"Trust in the LORD with all your heart, and do not lean on your own understanding. In all your ways acknowledge him, and he will make your paths straight."

- PROVERBS 3:5-6

A young man named Aaron was navigating the complex world of relationships during his college years. Like many of you, Aaron desired a meaningful and God-honoring relationship, but he was unsure of how to proceed.

One day, Aaron met a girl who seemed perfect on the surface. She was attractive, popular, and shared some common interests. However, something in Aaron's heart didn't feel quite right. He found himself wrestling with doubts and uncertainties.

In the midst of his confusion, Aaron turned to prayer. He sought God's guidance and asked for wisdom and discernment. He surrendered his desires and asked God to align his path with His will. Through prayer, Aaron learned to trust in the Lord with all his heart, recognizing that his own understanding might be limited.

As Aaron continued to seek God's guidance, he began to notice certain red flags in the relationship. He realized that they had different values and goals, and their faith wasn't aligned as he had hoped. It became clear to Aaron that God was showing him the importance of discernment and being intentional in his pursuit of a relationship.

Through this experience, Aaron learned a valuable lesson about seeking God's guidance in relationships. He discovered that prayer is a powerful tool for gaining wisdom and discernment. When we acknowledge God in all our ways and trust Him wholeheartedly, He will make our paths straight.

The story of Aaron teaches us the significance of seeking God's guidance in our romantic pursuits. It reminds us that outward appearances and common interests are not enough to build a lasting and fulfilling relationship. It is through prayer and seeking God's will that we can discern whether a relationship aligns with His plan and purpose for our lives.

Have you experienced a situation where you felt uncertain about a romantic relationship? How did you handle it?

How can prayer help you gain wisdom and discernment in your relationships?

Reflect on Proverbs 3:5-6. How can you apply the principles of trusting in the Lord and acknowledging Him in your romantic pursuits?

Prayer:

Dear God,

Thank You for the privilege of seeking Your guidance in all aspects of our lives, including relationships. Grant us wisdom and discernment as we navigate the complexities of dating and pursuing meaningful connections. Help us to trust in You with all our hearts and to acknowledge You in all our ways. May Your will be done in our relationships, and may we find joy and fulfillment in aligning our romantic pursuits with Your purpose.

Amen.

60

---◆○◆---

BUILDING EMOTIONAL
INTIMACY

_____ / _____ / _____

"Above all, love each other deeply, because love covers over a multitude of sins."

- I PETER 4:8

E motional intimacy is the foundation of a strong and fulfilling relationship. It requires trust, vulnerability, and a willingness to invest in understanding and supporting your partner. Trust is built over time through consistent actions, reliability, and open communication. It allows both partners to feel safe, valued, and accepted.

Vulnerability plays a crucial role in building emotional intimacy. It means being open and honest about your thoughts, feelings, and fears. It requires courage to share your deepest emotions and insecurities, knowing that your partner will listen without judgment and offer support. When both partners are vulnerable, a deeper connection and understanding can flourish.

To deepen emotional intimacy, prioritize quality time together. Create opportunities for meaningful conversations, where you can discuss your dreams, goals, and fears. Actively listen to your partner, show empathy, and be present in the moment. This builds a sense of closeness and strengthens the emotional bond between you.

The verse from 1 Peter 4:8 reminds us of the power of love in covering over a multitude of sins. It encourages us to love each other deeply, which includes demonstrating empathy, forgiveness, and grace in our relationships. As you build emotional intimacy, remember to extend love and understanding to your partner.

Building emotional intimacy takes time and effort. It requires intentional actions such as active listening, validating your partner's emotions, and expressing love and appreciation. It is an ongoing process of learning and growing together.

Reflect on your current level of emotional intimacy in your relationships. How can you cultivate more trust and vulnerability?

How does the verse from 1 Peter 4:8 inspire you to deepen your emotional connection with your partner?

Are there any fears or barriers that prevent you from being vulnerable in your relationships? How can you overcome them?

Prayer:

Dear God,

We thank You for the gift of emotional intimacy. Help us build trust, embrace vulnerability, and deepen our connections with our partners. May our relationships be rooted in love, understanding, and growth. Grant us the wisdom to invest in building emotional intimacy and create a strong foundation for our relationships.

Amen.

61

HEALTHY VS. UNHEALTHY RELATIONSHIPS

____ / ____ / _____

"Do not be yoked together with unbelievers. For what do righteousness and wickedness have in common? Or what fellowship can light have with darkness?"

- 2 CORINTHIANS 6:14

As someone who has walked the path of relationships and dating, I want to share valuable lessons with you about healthy and unhealthy relationships. It is crucial to recognize the red flags and seek God's best for your romantic partnerships.

In college, I experienced both healthy and unhealthy relationships. Looking back, I realize that the healthy relationships were characterized by mutual respect, trust, and a shared commitment to God's principles. On the other hand, the unhealthy relationships were marked by manipulation, disrespect, and a lack of shared values.

Recognizing red flags in a relationship is essential. It could be patterns of control, emotional or physical abuse, or a lack of accountability. These are signs that the relationship is veering off course and not aligning with God's best for you.

To navigate this, I encourage you to take ownership of your relationships. Seek God's guidance and wisdom through prayer and His Word. The verse from 2 Corinthians 6:14 reminds us not to be yoked together with unbelievers. While this verse primarily refers to marriage, it also highlights the importance of shared values and beliefs in a healthy relationship.

Take the time to get to know someone's character, observe how they treat others, and evaluate whether their values align with yours. Surround yourself with godly friends who can provide guidance and accountability in your relationship choices.

Remember, it's not about finding the perfect person, but about seeking God's best for you. Trust that He has someone who will walk alongside you, support you, and help you grow in your faith. Don't settle for less than what God desires for you.

Reflect on past relationships. Can you identify any red flags or signs of unhealthy dynamics? What have you learned from those experiences?

How does the verse from 2 Corinthians 6:14 guide your understanding of healthy relationships?

Are there any areas in your current relationships where you need to seek God's guidance and make necessary changes?

Prayer:

Dear God,

We seek Your wisdom and discernment in our relationships. Help us recognize red flags and make choices that align with Your will. Guide us to healthy relationships that honor You and bring joy and growth. Grant us the strength to let go of relationships that are not in line with Your best for us.

Amen.

62

BALANCING FRIENDSHIPS AND ROMANTIC PURSUITS

___ / ___ / _____

"Two are better than one because they have a good return for their labor."

- ECCLESIASTES 4:9

L et me share a story with you about a young man named Felix who faced the challenge of balancing his social life and romantic pursuits during his college years. Felix was eager to explore new friendships and potentially find a meaningful romantic relationship, but he also cherished the friendships he had cultivated over the years.

As Felix started dating someone, he noticed a shift in his priorities. He found himself spending most of his time with his new romantic interest, unintentionally neglecting his friends. Gradually, his social circle began to feel distant and disconnected.

One day, Felix realized the importance of maintaining healthy friendships alongside his romantic endeavors. He understood that friendships play a crucial role in our lives, offering support, companionship, and shared experiences. He also recognized that neglecting his friendships could lead to a sense of isolation and a loss of valuable connections.

Felix decided to take intentional steps to balance his social life and romantic pursuits. He set aside specific times to spend with his friends, nurturing those relationships and creating meaningful memories. He learned to communicate openly with his partner, expressing his desire to maintain a healthy balance between their romantic relationship and his friendships.

Through this experience, Felix discovered that friendship and dating are not mutually exclusive but can coexist harmoniously. He learned the importance of managing his time effectively, honoring commitments to both his friends and his romantic partner. By striking a balance, Felix experienced the joy of meaningful friendships and a fulfilling romantic relationship.

The story of Felix teaches us the significance of balancing our social life and romantic pursuits. It reminds us that friendships are a precious gift and should not be overshadowed by our pursuit of romantic relationships. It is through maintaining healthy friendships that we can find support, encouragement, and a sense of belonging.

How do you currently balance your social life and romantic pursuits? Are there any areas where you feel you may be neglecting your friendships?

Why is it important to maintain healthy friendships while exploring romantic relationships?

Reflect on Ecclesiastes 4:9. How can this verse guide you in balancing your social life and romantic pursuits?

Prayer:

Dear God,

Thank You for the gift of friendships and romantic relationships. Help us to navigate the delicate balance between our social lives and our romantic pursuits. Give us wisdom to manage our time effectively, so we can nurture our friendships while also investing in meaningful romantic relationships. May we always cherish and value the friendships in our lives, understanding the importance of community and companionship.

Amen.

SETTING GOALS

63

GOAL SETTING AND
SELF-REFLECTION

___ / ___ / _____

"Commit to the Lord whatever you do, and he will establish your plans."

- PROVERBS 16:3

Setting goals and engaging in regular self-reflection is essential for personal development, achievement, and continuous improvement. As someone who has experienced the power of goal setting, I want to offer you guidance on charting your course for success.

Goal setting begins with a vision. Take time to reflect on your dreams, passions, and aspirations. What do you want to achieve during your college years and beyond? Align your goals with your values and purpose. Seek God's guidance in your goal-setting process, committing your plans to Him.

Once you have a vision, break it down into smaller, actionable goals. Set both short-term and long-term goals that are specific, measurable, achievable, relevant, and time-bound (SMART goals). This framework provides clarity and direction, helping you stay focused and motivated.

Regular self-reflection is crucial in the goal-setting journey. Take time to assess your progress, identify areas of growth, and make necessary adjustments. Self-reflection allows you to celebrate successes, learn from failures, and continually refine your goals.

Incorporate biblical principles into your goal setting. Seek wisdom from God's Word, aligning your goals with His will. Proverbs 16:3 reminds us to commit our plans to the Lord. Trust in His guidance and surrender your goals to Him, allowing Him to establish your path.

As you set goals and engage in self-reflection, remember that success is not solely measured by achievements but also by personal growth and character development. Embrace the journey and the lessons it brings.

What is your vision for your college years and beyond? How can your goals align with your purpose and values?

How can you break down your vision into SMART goals? Are there any adjustments you need to make?

How can you incorporate regular self-reflection into your goal-setting process? What lessons have you learned through self-reflection so far?

Prayer:

Dear God,

We commit our plans and goals to You. Guide us in setting meaningful goals and engaging in regular self-reflection. Help us align our ambitions with Your will and purpose. Grant us the strength, wisdom, and perseverance to pursue our goals and grow in character along the way.

Amen.

———◆◇◆———

64

DEVELOPING A GROWTH MINDSET

____ / ____ / _____

"I can do all things through him who strengthens me."

- PHILIPPIANS 4:13

D uring college life, it is essential to develop a growth mindset—a mindset of resilience, embracing challenges, and pursuing personal growth. Let me share a story that taught me the power of a growth mindset.

I once knew a college student named Isaac. He was passionate about computer programming but struggled with a challenging coding project. Frustration started to creep in, and he felt like giving up. However, Isaac decided to adopt a growth mindset and see the challenge as an opportunity to learn and improve.

Instead of viewing setbacks as failures, Isaac embraced them as stepping stones to success. He sought help from his professors and fellow students, who provided guidance and support. He spent extra hours in the library, studying coding techniques and exploring different approaches. With each hurdle he overcame, Isaac's confidence grew, and he realized the value of perseverance and embracing challenges.

Through this experience, Isaac learned that personal growth and achievement come from stepping out of his comfort zone and embracing the unknown. He discovered that failures and setbacks were not indicators of his worth but opportunities for growth and learning. By developing a growth mindset, Isaac transformed challenges into opportunities and achieved remarkable success in his coding projects.

The story of Isaac teaches us the power of a growth mindset in overcoming challenges and achieving personal growth. It reminds us to embrace setbacks as opportunities for learning, seek support and guidance, and persevere in the face of difficulties. With a growth mindset, we can unlock our full potential and achieve remarkable success in our pursuits.

In what areas of your life do you struggle to embrace challenges? How can you adopt a growth mindset in those areas?

Reflect on a recent setback or failure. How did you initially respond to it? How could a growth mindset have influenced your perspective and actions?

How can you cultivate a mindset of continuous learning and improvement? What steps can you take to embrace challenges and pursue personal growth?

Prayer:

Dear God,

Grant us the strength to develop a growth mindset. Help us embrace challenges and see them as opportunities for growth. Teach us to persevere, seek support, and approach difficulties with a mindset of resilience and determination. May we trust in Your power to strengthen us and guide us in our journey of personal growth.

Amen.

65

---◄O►---

START WITH SMALL AND
MEANINGFUL GOALS

___ / ___ / _____

"Where there is no vision, the people perish..."

- PROVERBS 29:18A (KJV)

S etting small and meaningful goals that align with your vision and purpose will help you to progress much further than you could imagine. Embracing the power of vision and purpose will shape your college experience and future endeavors.

Starting with small goals allows you to build momentum and confidence. Begin by identifying areas in your life where you want to grow, such as academics, personal relationships, faith, or physical health. Set achievable goals within these areas, focusing on progress rather than perfection.

Having a vision provides a sense of direction and purpose. Take time to reflect on your values, passions, and the impact you want to make in the world. Your college experience can serve as a stepping stone toward fulfilling that vision. Seek God's guidance in discovering your purpose, allowing Him to shape your goals.

Meaningful goals are those that resonate deeply with your values and align with God's principles. Consider how your goals can positively impact others, reflect your faith, and contribute to the greater good. By pursuing meaningful goals, you can experience a sense of fulfillment and purpose in your endeavors.

Remember to celebrate small victories along the way. Each step forward, no matter how small, brings you closer to your vision. Use setbacks as opportunities for growth and learning. Trust in God's faithfulness and His ability to guide you on your journey.

What areas of your life do you want to focus on for personal growth during your college years? How can you set small, achievable goals within those areas?

How does having a vision and purpose influence your goal-setting process? How can your goals align with your faith and values?

Reflect on a small goal you recently achieved. How did it contribute to your overall vision? How can you celebrate and build upon that success?

Prayer:

Dear God,

We thank You for the power of vision and purpose. Guide us in setting small and meaningful goals that align with Your will and honor You. Grant us clarity, determination, and resilience as we pursue our dreams. May our goals bring positive change in our lives and in the lives of others.

Amen.

66

OVERCOMING OBSTACLES

____ / ____ / _____

"Be strong and courageous. Do not be afraid or terrified because of
them, for the Lord your God goes with you; he will never leave you
nor forsake you."

- DEUTERONOMY 31:6

Throughout your college journey, you will encounter obstacles
and adversities that may test your resolve. In these moments, it
is crucial to overcome obstacles, persevere, and rely on God's strength.
Let me share an inspiring story that taught me the power of resilience.

There was a student named Benjamin. He was passionate about playing the piano and dreamed of participating in a prestigious music
competition. However, just weeks before the event, he injured his
hand, making it challenging to play. Benjamin faced a difficult decision—to give up on his dream or persevere through the pain and
uncertainty.

Instead of succumbing to discouragement, Benjamin chose to rely on
God's strength and trust His plan. He sought medical attention and

diligently followed the prescribed rehabilitation program. It was a long and arduous journey, filled with doubts and setbacks. Yet, Benjamin clung to his faith and found solace in God's promise to never leave nor forsake him.

Through unwavering determination, Benjamin gradually regained his piano-playing abilities. He practiced tirelessly, even when progress seemed slow. As the competition day approached, he stood on stage, nervous yet filled with gratitude for the journey that had led him there. Benjamin's performance was a testament to his perseverance and reliance on God's strength.

This story teaches us that overcoming obstacles requires resilience, seeking support, and trusting in God's faithfulness. Adversities may come in various forms—a difficult course, a challenging relationship, or personal struggles—but with God's presence and our determination, we can persevere and rise above.

Think about a recent obstacle or adversity you faced. How did you respond to it? How can you incorporate resilience and reliance on God's strength in such situations?

Reflect on a time when you overcame a significant challenge. What strategies did you employ, and how did God's presence sustain you?

How can you seek support during difficult times? Who are the people in your life whom you can rely on for encouragement and guidance?

Prayer:

Dear God,

We thank You for Your promise to be with us through every obstacle and adversity. Grant us the strength to persevere, the wisdom to seek support, and the faith to trust in Your plan. Help us rely on Your strength and find solace in Your presence. May we overcome challenges and adversities with resilience and unwavering faith.

Amen.

67

---◆◇◆---

CELEBRATING MILESTONES

_____ / _____ / _____

"This is the day that the Lord has made; let us rejoice and be glad in it."

- PSALM 118:24

As you progress through your college journey, it is important to take moments to celebrate milestones, express gratitude, and reflect on the journey. Let me share a story that highlights the value of celebrating milestones and finding joy in the journey.

Liam embarked on his college experience with dreams and aspirations, but the journey was not without challenges and setbacks. However, Liam chose to approach each day with gratitude, embracing both the successes and the failures as opportunities for growth.

Along the way, Liam set small goals for himself—completing a challenging course, participating in extracurricular activities, or making new friends. With each milestone reached, he took time to reflect on his achievements, express gratitude for the progress made, and offer thanks to God for His guidance.

Liam found joy not only in the destination but also in the journey itself. He learned to appreciate the moments of learning, the connections formed with fellow students, and the personal development that occurred along the way. Celebrating milestones became a way for him to acknowledge God's faithfulness and recognize the progress made, regardless of the size or significance of the achievement.

Through Liam's story, we learn the importance of celebrating milestones, expressing gratitude, and finding joy in the journey. Each day is a gift from God, and every step taken is an opportunity to grow closer to Him and fulfill His purpose for our lives.

Think about a recent milestone or achievement in your college journey. How did you celebrate it? How can you incorporate gratitude and reflection into your celebrations?

Reflect on the small victories and progress you've made along the way. How can you find joy in the everyday moments of your college experience?

How can you express gratitude to God for His guidance and faithfulness throughout your journey? In what ways can you cultivate a spirit of thankfulness?

Prayer:

Dear God,

We thank You for the milestones we have achieved and the journey You have led us on. Teach us to celebrate each step, expressing gratitude and finding joy in the process. Help us appreciate the small victories and reflect on the progress made. May our hearts be filled with thankfulness for Your guidance and faithfulness.

Amen.

68

MANAGING EXPECTATIONS

____ / ____ / _____

"Commit your work to the Lord, and your plans will be established."

- PROVERBS 16:3

In college, it's common to feel the pressure to excel academically, pursue extracurricular activities, and set high aspirations for your future. While ambition is commendable, it's crucial to strike a balance and set goals that are both challenging and attainable.

When I was in college, I had lofty ambitions and desired to accomplish great things. However, I soon realized the importance of managing my expectations and being realistic about my limitations. It was a lesson learned through experience and seeking God's guidance.

You see, taking ownership of your education means understanding your strengths and weaknesses, acknowledging your capacity, and setting goals that align with your abilities. It's about finding the sweet spot where ambition meets practicality.

It's important to remember that setting unrealistic goals can lead to frustration, burnout, and a sense of failure. On the other hand, setting goals that are too easily attainable may limit your growth and hinder your potential. The key is to find the middle ground—a place where you can stretch yourself while maintaining a healthy balance.

By committing your work to the Lord and seeking His guidance, you can set goals that are aligned with His purpose for your life. It's essential to involve God in your goal-setting process, seeking His wisdom, and asking Him to help you discern the right path.

As you navigate college life, take time to reflect on your ambitions, evaluate your expectations, and seek God's guidance. Embrace progress over perfection and celebrate the small victories along the way. Remember, God has a unique plan for your life, and He will establish your plans as you commit them to Him.

Reflect on your current goals and expectations. Are they balanced between ambition and realism? How can you adjust them to align with your abilities and God's purpose for your life?

Have you ever experienced the consequences of setting unrealistic goals? How can you learn from those experiences and manage your expectations more effectively?

In what ways can you involve God in your goal-setting process? How can you seek His wisdom and guidance as you make decisions about your education and future?

Prayer:

Dear God,

We thank You for the guidance You provide as we navigate our college journey. Help us find a balance between ambition and realism in setting our goals. Teach us to commit our work to You and seek Your wisdom. Guide us in managing our expectations and finding joy in the progress we make.

Amen.

GRADUATING WITH A KINGDOM MINDSET

69

EXPLORING CAREER PATHS

_____ / _____ / _____

*"For I know the plans I have for you," declares the Lord, "plans to prosper
you and not to harm you, plans to give you hope and a future."*

- JEREMIAH 29:11

As you approach graduation, the question of career options and discovering your calling may weigh heavily on your mind. Let me share some insights to guide you in navigating this important phase of your life.

The transition from college to the professional world can be both exciting and overwhelming. You may find yourself pondering various career options, wondering which path to pursue. It is during this time that the process of self-discovery becomes crucial.

God has a unique plan for each one of us. He has placed within us talents, passions, and interests that can guide us toward fulfilling our purpose. As you explore different career options, it is essential to engage in a process of self-discovery.

Take time to reflect on your strengths, values, and the activities that bring you joy. Consider the skills you have developed during your college journey and how they can be applied in various professional fields. Explore different industries and seek opportunities to gain insights and experiences that will help you discern your calling.

Research different career paths and seek guidance from mentors, professors, and professionals in your fields of interest. They can provide valuable insights and advice to help you make informed decisions. Additionally, seek counsel from God through prayer, asking Him to reveal His plans and align your desires with His purpose for your life.

Remember that discovering your calling is not always a linear journey. It may involve taking detours, trying new things, and even facing challenges along the way. Embrace these experiences as opportunities for growth and learning.

As you explore career options, keep in mind that your ultimate goal should be to align your work with God's kingdom purposes. Whether you pursue a career in business, healthcare, education, or any other field, seek ways to use your skills and talents to make a positive impact, serve others, and glorify God.

Be open to God's leading and trust that He will guide you to the path that is best suited for you. His plans are to prosper you, give you hope, and provide a future filled with purpose and fulfillment.

What are your strengths, passions, and interests? How can you align them with potential career options?

How can you engage in self-discovery and gain insights into your calling? Are there specific experiences or opportunities you can pursue?

How can you seek guidance from mentors, professionals, and God Himself as you navigate career options?

In what ways can you use your career to serve others and make a positive impact for God's kingdom?

Prayer:

Dear God,

As we embark on the journey of exploring career options, we seek Your guidance and wisdom. Open our hearts and minds to discover our calling and align our desires with Your purpose. Help us use our skills and talents to make a positive impact and bring glory to Your name. Lead us on the path that leads to fulfillment and purpose.

Amen.

70

EMBRACING LIFE LONG LEARNING

___ / ___ / _____

"Whatever you do, work at it with all your heart, as working for the Lord, not for human masters."

- COLOSSIANS 3:23

As you prepare to graduate and step into the professional world, remember the importance of embracing lifelong learning. The world is constantly evolving, and to thrive in your career, you must commit to continuous growth and development. Seek opportunities to enhance your skills, both personally and professionally, and adapt to the changing job market.

Building transferable skills is vital in today's dynamic workforce. These are skills that can be applied across various industries and roles, making you versatile and valuable. Acquire a diverse skill set that includes communication, problem-solving, adaptability, leadership, and critical thinking. These skills will serve as a strong foundation for your future endeavors, enabling you to navigate different career paths.

By approaching your learning journey with a Kingdom mindset, you recognize that all your efforts are dedicated to the Lord. View education and skill development as an act of worship, using your talents and abilities to honor God and make a positive impact in the world. Embrace the opportunity to continuously grow, not only for personal gain but also to serve others with excellence.

How can you seek opportunities for personal and professional development during your college years and beyond?

What are some transferable skills that you possess or would like to acquire? How can they benefit you in different career paths?

How can you view your educational journey as an act of worship, dedicated to serving God and others with excellence?

Prayer:

Dear God,

Thank you for the gift of education and the opportunity to continuously learn and grow. Help me embrace lifelong learning and seek opportunities to develop my skills. Grant me the wisdom to adapt to a changing job market and use my abilities to honor you in all that I do. Guide me as I build transferable skills that will enable me to make a positive impact in my future career.

Amen.

71

Networking and Professional Relationships

___ / ___ / _____

"Iron sharpens iron, and one man sharpens another."

-Proverbs 27:17

Imagine yourself entering the professional world after graduating from college. You have a degree in hand, a passion for your chosen field, and a desire to make a meaningful impact. However, you quickly realize that success is not achieved in isolation. As you navigate your career path, you come to understand the importance of networking and cultivating professional relationships.

In college, you may have had the opportunity to connect with classmates, professors, and professionals in your field during internships or networking events. These encounters allowed you to sharpen your skills, gain valuable insights, and expand your horizons. However, as you enter the working world, the significance of these connections becomes even more evident.

You meet Jonathan, a seasoned professional who is passionate about mentoring young graduates like yourself. He takes you under his wing, offering guidance, sharing industry knowledge, and introducing you to influential individuals in your field. Through Jonathan's mentorship, you realize that networking is not just about collecting business cards or adding contacts on social media; it is about cultivating genuine connections and fostering relationships that can propel your career forward.

Jonathan teaches you the art of networking with integrity and authenticity. He emphasizes the value of reciprocity and encourages you to approach networking as an opportunity to contribute and add value to others' lives, rather than solely seeking personal gain. Together, you attend conferences, industry events, and networking gatherings, where you meet like-minded professionals who share your passion and aspirations. These encounters lead to collaborations, job opportunities, and lifelong friendships.

Through this journey, you learn that networking is not a self-serving endeavor but a way to build a supportive community that uplifts and encourages one another. You realize the power of surrounding yourself with individuals who challenge you, inspire you, and help you grow both personally and professionally.

How can you actively build and maintain professional relationships during your college years?

What steps can you take to network with integrity and authenticity?

How can you contribute and add value to the lives of others in your professional network?

Take a moment to reflect on these prompts and consider how you can cultivate connections for career growth as you graduate with a Kingdom mindset.

Prayer:

Dear God,

Thank you for the gift of networking and the opportunity to connect with others in our chosen fields. Help us approach networking with integrity and authenticity, seeking to contribute and add value to the lives of those we encounter. Guide us in building and maintaining meaningful professional relationships that will not only benefit our careers but also align with your purpose for our lives.

Amen.

PURSUING INTERNSHIPS AND EXPERIENTIAL LEARNING

____ / ____ / _____

"Commit to the LORD whatever you do, and he will establish your plans."

— PROVERBS 16:3

As you journey through college and prepare for your future career, it's crucial to recognize the value of internships and experiential learning. These opportunities provide practical experience that goes beyond the classroom, contributing to your personal growth, skill development, and career exploration.

Internships offer a unique chance to apply your academic knowledge in real-world settings. They provide hands-on experience, allowing you to see the practical implications of what you have learned and discover how different industries operate. Through internships, you can develop new skills, gain industry insights, and build a network of professional contacts.

Experiential learning goes beyond internships and includes activities such as research projects, service-learning, and leadership roles on campus. These experiences offer opportunities for personal growth, as they challenge you to step outside your comfort zone, develop problem-solving skills, and learn from both successes and failures. They contribute to your holistic development and help shape your career aspirations.

When pursuing internships and engaging in experiential learning, commit your efforts to the Lord. Seek His guidance and trust that He will establish your plans. Approach these experiences with humility, eagerness to learn, and a servant's heart. Recognize that God can use these opportunities to shape your character, open doors, and align your path with His purpose for your life.

How can you actively pursue internships and experiential learning opportunities during your college journey?

What skills and insights do you hope to gain from these experiences? How can they contribute to your career exploration?

In what ways can you approach internships and experiential learning with a humble and servant-hearted attitude, seeking to honor God in all that you do?

Prayer:

Dear Lord,

Thank you for the opportunities of internships and experiential learning that lie before me. Guide me as I seek practical experiences that will shape my skills, broaden my horizons, and help me discern my career path. Help me approach these opportunities with humility, eager to learn and serve others. I commit my plans to you, trusting that you will establish them according to your purpose.

Amen.

73

DEALING WITH UNCERTAINTY

____ / ____ / _____

"Trust in the LORD with all your heart, and do not lean on your own understanding. In all your ways acknowledge him, and he will make straight your paths."

-PROVERBS 3:5-6

Imagine yourself at a crossroads in your career journey. You have been presented with a new opportunity, but it means leaving behind the familiar and stepping into the unknown. This transition brings a sense of uncertainty and apprehension. In times like these, it is crucial to trust in God's guidance and seek His wisdom.

As you reflect on Proverbs 3:5-6, you realize that God invites you to trust Him wholeheartedly, even when the path ahead seems unclear. He encourages you to rely on His understanding rather than leaning solely on your own limited perspective. This is a humbling realization, as it requires surrendering control and acknowledging that God's plans are higher than our own.

You recall the story of Abraham, who was called to leave his homeland

and go to a land God would show him. Abraham faced uncertainty and had to trust in God's guidance step by step. Despite not knowing the destination, Abraham's faith in God led him to incredible blessings and a legacy that impacted generations.

In your own life, you may encounter moments of career transitions where uncertainty weighs heavy on your heart. It is during these times that you are called to surrender your plans and trust in God's perfect timing and guidance. Through prayer and seeking His wisdom, you can navigate the unknown with confidence, knowing that God goes before you and has a purpose for every season of your life.

Trusting in God's guidance does not mean that all uncertainty will vanish or that the path will always be smooth. However, it means that you can have peace in the midst of uncertainty, knowing that God is faithful and will direct your steps as you align your plans with His will.

How can you actively trust in God's guidance during career transitions?

What steps can you take to seek God's wisdom and discern His plans for your life?

How does relying on God's understanding rather than leaning on your own understanding bring peace and clarity in times of uncertainty?

Take a moment to reflect on these prompts and consider how you can trust God's guidance in navigating career transitions and embracing His plans for your life.

Prayer:

Dear God,

Thank you for your faithfulness and guidance in every aspect of our lives, including our careers. Help us to trust in you wholeheartedly, especially during times of uncertainty and transitions. Grant us wisdom and discernment as we seek your will and align our plans with yours. May we find peace in knowing that you go before us and have a purpose for every season of our lives.

Amen.

74

GRADUATING WITH A KINGDOM MINDSET

____ / ____ / _____

*"Whatever you do, work at it with all your heart, as working for the
Lord, not for human masters."*

- COLOSSIANS 3:23

As you approach the end of your college journey and step into
the working world, it's essential to graduate with a Kingdom
mindset. This mindset involves infusing your faith into your professional life, using your talents and skills for God's glory, and making a
positive impact in the world around you.

Remember that your career is not just about earning a paycheck or
climbing the corporate ladder. It's an opportunity to be a light for
Christ in your workplace, to bring His love, compassion, and integrity
into your interactions with colleagues, clients, and customers. Your
job becomes a platform to showcase the transformative power of the
Gospel.

Infuse your faith into your professional life by seeking wisdom and guidance from God in your decision-making, relying on His strength in challenging times, and living out your values with integrity. Let your actions and attitudes reflect your commitment to following Christ, and be willing to share your faith when appropriate, allowing others to witness the hope that resides within you.

Furthermore, use your talents and skills as tools for God's glory. Recognize that He has equipped you with unique abilities and passions for a purpose. Seek opportunities to serve others, to make a positive impact in your field of work, and to be an advocate for justice, mercy, and righteousness.

As you embark on this new chapter, remember that your career is not the ultimate goal but a means to serve God and others. Seek to make a lasting impact in the lives of those around you, sharing the love of Christ through your words and actions. Let your work be a reflection of your dedication to excellence, honesty, and servant leadership.

In conclusion, graduating with a Kingdom mindset means integrating your faith into your career, using your talents for God's glory, and making a positive impact in the world. As you step into the working world, remember that your purpose extends beyond your job title. You are called to be an ambassador for Christ, carrying His light into every aspect of your life. Trust in His guidance, lean on His strength, and strive to impact the world for Christ through your career.

How can you infuse your faith into your professional life? In what practical ways can you demonstrate Christ-like values and attitudes in your workplace?

Reflect on the talents and skills God has given you. How can you use them to bring glory to God and make a positive impact in your chosen career path?

Reflect on the ultimate goal of your career. How can you shift your perspective to view it as a means to serve God and others, rather than solely focusing on personal success or advancement?

Think about specific ways you can make a positive impact in the lives of those around you through your work. How can you share the love of Christ through your words, actions, and willingness to serve others?

Prayer:

Dear Heavenly Father,

I thank you for the journey of college and the preparation it has provided me for the working world. As I graduate, I pray that you infuse my heart with a Kingdom mindset. Help me to see my career as an opportunity to honor you, to use my talents for your glory, and to impact the world around me. Guide me, Lord, in making wise decisions, in demonstrating integrity, and in sharing your love with others. May my life be a testament to your faithfulness and grace.

Amen.

THE AFTERWORD

WHERE ONE STORY ENDS, ANOTHER BEGINS

Congratulations on reaching the end of this book! I sincerely hope that it has been a valuable companion on your college journey. As you reflect on the pages you've read, I encourage you to take a moment to pause and contemplate the lessons you've learned, the wisdom you've gained, and the growth you've experienced.

Remember, the college years are just the beginning of a lifelong adventure. The knowledge and insights you've acquired here will serve as a foundation for your future endeavors. As you move forward, embrace the opportunities and challenges that await you, knowing that you are equipped with the tools to navigate them with confidence and purpose.

I want to express my deepest gratitude to you for choosing this book and allowing me to be a part of your college experience. As a self-publisher, every reader's support means the world to me. Your engagement with the content and your willingness to learn from my experiences reaffirm my purpose in sharing these words.

If you found this book valuable and impactful, I kindly ask for your support by leaving a review. Reviews play a crucial role in helping self-published authors like myself reach a wider audience. Your honest review will not only make my day but also contribute to the growth of this book and future projects, as well as assist other readers deciding to embark on their own transformative college journeys.

You can easily leave a review by scanning the QR code below or by searching for "Biblical Teachings" on Amazon. Additionally, I invite you to explore my other books on Amazon, where you can find further insights and teachings to deepen your faith and personal growth.

Customer reviews
★★★★½ 4.6 out of 5

Review this product
Share your thoughts with other customers

Write a customer review

Thank you once again for your readership, and may your college years continue to be filled with growth, joy, and endless possibilities!